"The competent craftsperson should be equal to a professor in philosophy – both disciplines are rich, deep, and complex."

– Jögge Sundqvist

MORTISE & TENON
magazine

JOSHUA A. KLEIN
Editor-in-Chief
Designer

MICHAEL UPDEGRAFF
Editorial Assistant

JIM MCCONNELL
Content Editor

MEGAN FITZPATRICK
Content & Copy Editor

© 2019 *Mortise & Tenon Magazine*

All rights reserved. No part of this publication may be reproduced in any form or by any means including electronic and mechanical methods, without prior written permission from the publisher, except in the case of brief quotations in critical reviews and certain noncommercial uses permitted by copyright law.

Send all inquiries to:
info@mortiseandtenonmag.com

To subscribe, visit:
www.mortiseandtenonmag.com

Mortise & Tenon Magazine
14 Porcupine Ln
Sedgwick, ME 04676

Printed in the United States of America

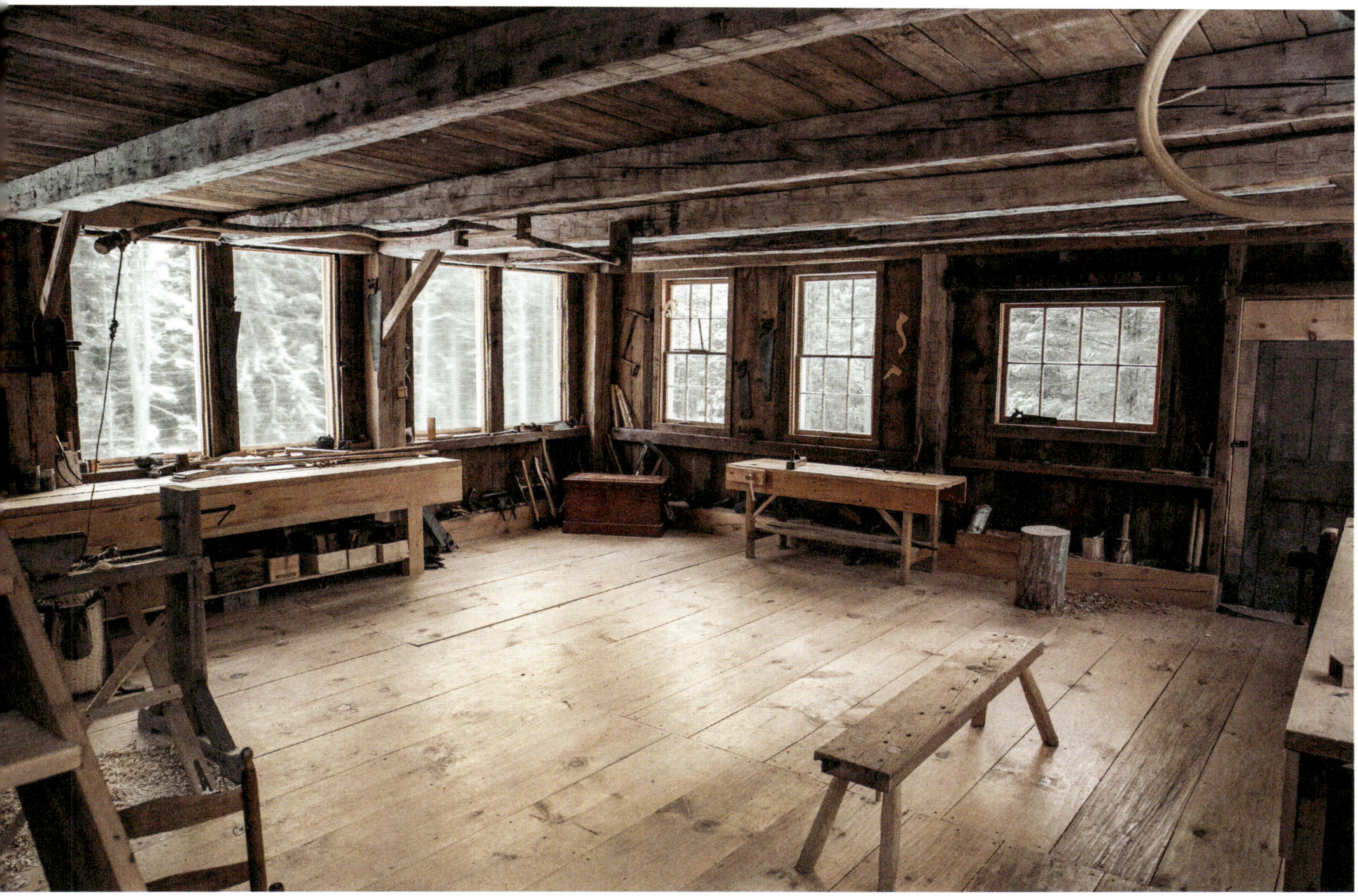

CONTRIBUTORS

Steve Voigt makes traditional wooden planes in his shop in Allentown, Pennsylvania. He uses a few basic power tools for rough dimensioning, but the majority of work is done by hand, much as it would have been more than 200 years ago. Steve has written for *Popular Woodworking Magazine* as well as his blog, *The Black Dog's Woodshop*. His work has been profiled by Christopher Schwarz, Don Williams, and others. Steve's current projects include expanding his line of planes and finishing some long-delayed furniture for his very patient wife.

Nathaniel Brewster is fascinated by the history of woodworking – its tools, techniques, and people. A perpetually aspiring woodworker, he is slowly filling his home with the results of his experimentation with the craft. He lives with his wife and two children outside of Boston.

David Lane is a woodworker and former librarian. Lane graduated from Columbia University's School of Library Service in 1981 and has worked in the Memphis, Tennessee; Kansas City, Kansas; and Minneapolis, Minnesota library systems. Lane has published in *American Libraries* and *Woodwork* magazines. His woodwork has been exhibited at the Minnesota *Northern Woods Exhibition* annually since 2005.

Michael Updegraff is editorial assistant at *M&T*, a role which encompasses such diverse tasks as tracking down ideas for future articles, practicing photography and video work, sharpening slöjd knives, ensuring the proper use of the Oxford Comma (such as the following), and milking goats. His previous work experiences include carpentry, boatbuilding, and fishing on a lobster boat. He lives in the woods with his wife and three children, where they enjoy exploring, stacking firewood, learning traditional handcrafts, and listening for owls at night.

Jim McConnell has an insatiable curiosity and learns something new practically every day. As a husband and father of three precocious daughters, his days are full of unanticipated opportunities for love and grace. He currently resides in eastern North Carolina, and works for the peace and prosperity of the community in which he lives. He is a contributing editor for *Mortise & Tenon Magazine* and has also written for *Popular Woodworking Magazine*. He enjoys building furniture in his garage workshop, and although he prefers the simple to the ornate, he enjoys making useful things that are also occasionally beautiful.

Joshua A. Klein is editor-in-chief of *Mortise & Tenon Magazine* and has been published by *American Period Furniture* and *Popular Woodworking Magazine*. Joshua has been selected every year since 2015 for the Early American Life Directory of Traditional American Crafts for his hand-tool-only approach to period furniture making. He is the author of *Hands Employed Aright: The Furniture Making of Jonathan Fisher (1768-1847)* (Lost Art Press, 2018). Joshua, with his wife and three sons, is currently restoring a 200-year-old cape while homesteading on the coast of Maine, always with an eye to learn from his cultural heritage.

Brock Jobe holds the title of professor of American decorative arts emeritus at the Winterthur Museum after a lengthy teaching career in the Winterthur Program in American Material Culture, as well as earlier curatorial positions at the Museum of Fine Arts, Boston; Colonial Williamsburg; and Historic New England. He has authored or edited seven books, the most recent of which, *Crafting Excellence: The Furniture of Nathan Lumbard and His Circle*, he co-authored with Christie Jackson and Clark Pearce. Brock serves on the boards of Old Sturbridge Village and the Decorative Arts Trust, and still retains an office at Winterthur, where he continues to study, write, and lecture about American furniture.

Wilbur Pan lives in New Jersey, and is the author of the *Giant Cypress* blog (www.giantcypress.net). He has long been interested in understanding the use of Japanese woodworking tools. He has written articles for *Popular Woodworking Magazine*, and filmed a video on Japanese tools for Popular Woodworking. He has given talks on Japanese tools at Woodworking in America, Kezurou Kai USA, World Maker Faire New York, and many other venues.

Arsenios Hill makes his home in the Sonoran Desert of Arizona, along with his wife and their seven children. He grew up in the rainforest of South America and currently works as an educator. His adventurous past includes lots of rock climbing, whitewater rafting, fly fishing, blacksmithing, and, lately, wood carving. He also, with his family, manages a mini-farm with goats, ducks, and chickens.

TABLE *of* CONTENTS
ISSUE VI

8	The Good Life: Discussing Slöjd with Jögge Sundqvist
26	Cutting-edge Technology: Rediscovering the Double-iron Plane STEVE VOIGT
36	A Chair Called Henry NATHANIEL BREWSTER
44	William Morris & George Nakashima: Finding the Middle Landscape DAVID LANE
56	Examination of an 1804 Painted Cupboard
66	A Tale of Two Trees: The Radical Efficiency of Green Woodworking MICHAEL UPDEGRAFF
84	A Painted Chest in the Pennsylvania-German Tradition JIM MCCONNELL
96	The Wooden Brace: Bitstock Technology for the 21st Century JOSHUA A. KLEIN
114	The Cabinetmaker's Shop: Breathing New Life into an Old Trade BROCK JOBE
128	Forging Traditions: The Common Ancestry of Japanese & Western Edge Tools WILBUR PAN
138	Book Recommendation: *The Unknown Craftsman* ARSENIOS HILL

"Good workmanship – that is, careful, considerate, and loving work – requires us to think considerately of the whole process, natural and cultural, involved in the making of wooden artifacts…"

– Wendell Berry

FROM THE EDITOR

Woodworkers are uniquely positioned in 21st-century society. Though we may be participants in all that modern technology offers us, our time in the shop seems to be something from another world. Today, even the simple practice of making something with our own two hands is often cast as quaint – possibly even regressive.

But modernity has no monopoly on insight.

Many of us spend our entire workday sitting down while staring at computer screens. Our backs are incessantly sore, our wrists seize up, and our stress levels are through the roof. The belief that the "Information Era" has liberated the worker from the drudgery of manual labor is, at best, an overstatement. Just ask your chiropractor; we were not designed to be sedentary creatures.

To compensate for our professional inactivity, many of us go for a run or hike to get our blood flowing again. The reason leisure time in modern, urban life is often a retreat into nature for physical activity is because we all know it's good for us to sweat once in a while.

During our visit, Jögge Sundqvist told us, "Slöjd [craft] makes my body strong, gives me a strong back and muscles – slöjd contains a rich diet for both body and mind. Also, I'm able to repair things when they break. That's why I think of it as a survival kit – in a society where we're trying to be sustainable and live more simply, craft can be a part of that restoration."

This idea, that craftwork can provide a sense of wholeness, self-reliance, and joy, pervades this issue. Between Mike Updegraff's look at the "radical efficiency" of sourcing your own lumber, my own exploration into making your own wooden brace, and the connections David Lane draws between William Morris' and George Nakashima's emphases on craftsmanship over against the machine, the theme of independence and artisanal competence resounds.

Even the whimsy of the Windsor chair in Nathaniel Brewster's article, the Pennsylvania cupboard photo examination, and Jim McConnell's own expression from this tradition all point to the individuality of the maker and the joy of making, heedless of cultural convention.

This issue brings together so many interesting threads that I never envisioned woven together. And as we dug into our authors' work, Mike commented that he has never before been so struck by the immediate and future relevance of this craft tradition. We hope Issue Six broadens your perspective on working wood in the 21st century, even as it has for us.

Keep making shavings,

Joshua A. Klein
Editor

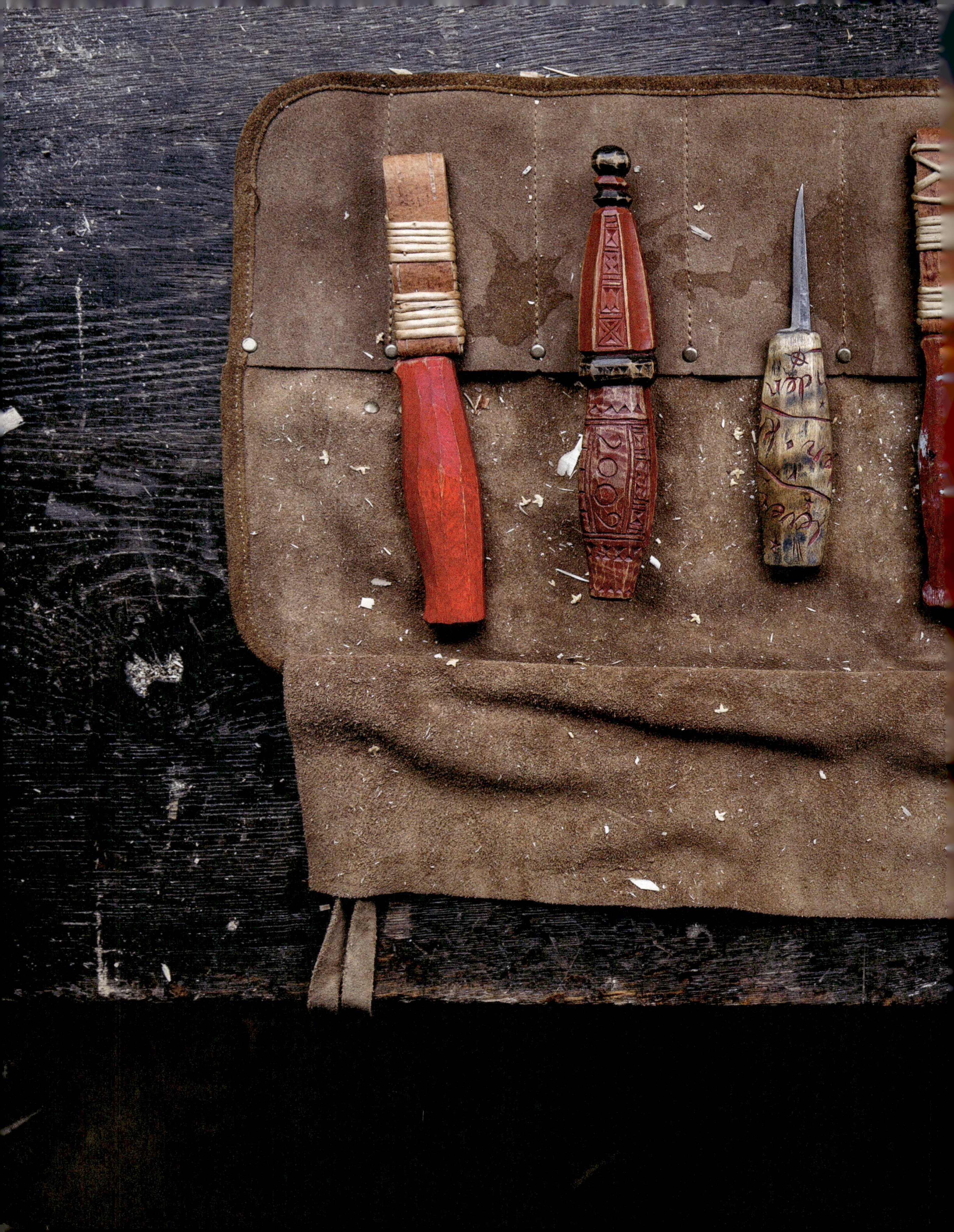

The GOOD LIFE

Discussing Slöjd *with* Jögge Sundqvist

Jögge Sundqvist has worked in the Swedish *slöjd* (pronounced "sloyd") tradition of woodworking since he was a child. Taught the craft by his father, Wille Sundqvist, Jögge works in green and dry wood that he sources from the forests around his home. He uses simple hand tools to create beautiful, whimsical, and practical objects that embrace traditional forms and explore the limits of sculpting in wood. Jögge's work has been featured in numerous publications and museums. He recently taught several classes at the Maine Coast Craft School, and we had the chance to sit down with him and talk about his work, his influences, and the future of handcraft.

Näve, Grace, Sign, Smack, and Face lt. Photo: Jostein Skeidsvoll.

M&T: We're grateful to have the chance to spend some time with you while you're here. Many folks in the U.S. are familiar with the word "slöjd," but there are some misconceptions about what it actually means. Can you unpack the idea for us?

JS: Slöjd is the Swedish word for "craft." It's an old word with Viking roots, and describes the manufacture of items made in the home for your own needs. People have been doing this for 20,000 years to survive – producing textiles, household goods, furniture, and the tools used for daily chores and transportation; they did it all by themselves. It's a mobile craft and so the tools can travel with you. By carrying just a few of them, you can make small items anywhere – it's freeing. You don't need a big workshop with a lot of power tools and accessories.

    In my part of Sweden, traditional slöjd is still something that people do, although the word is used in schools as a term for practical learning in a wider, more modern perspective. The root of the word slöjd is *slög*, which means practical or crafty – it describes someone who can take materials from where they live and put them together to make something useful. But we never call ourselves slög – we're so humble, you know – so we say that we're *int oslög*, not uncrafty, not unhandy. Though the younger generation may not get it, the older people in my country know exactly what I'm talking about.

    To understand my influences and the intellectual framework I use, I talk about slöjd in terms of the four walls of my workshop. There's the Materials wall, the Tool wall, the Tradition wall, and the Folk-Art wall. If you want to work with hand tools, you want the material to be superior – no twist, knots, or gnarly fibers. It must split well. I go out to the forest and find that one tree in 10,000 to have just the right material. This is so important in my workshop and it affects everything I do – the fibers and strength of the wood determine the design. The next wall is the Tool wall, which is also very important, and with it goes all the skills of how to grind a tool and how to use it in the process of working. I have a shave horse, a chopping block, a froe, some drills, some saws, many slöjd knives and axes, and I can

Woolbasket. Early 11th century. Nordiska Museet. Courtesy of Jögge Sundqvist.

make whatever I want within these walls.

The Tradition wall is super thick – about two meters thick – from 20,000 years of practicing, forgetting bad ideas, and keeping the good ideas. Practicing, practicing, and learning from one generation to the next: "Don't do it like that, do it like this." There is so much knowledge in tradition – details of knife grips, of the ways to spin a thread – but we've almost forgotten them today.

The fourth wall is the Folk-Art wall. Because I love colors, designs, and the beauty of objects, of course I had to have a relationship to art – function and art must go together. In my tradition of self-sufficiency, people never had any formal education at all, but they knew how to make a good scythe or axe handle and how to make a spinning wheel so it worked perfectly. And even though they were poor, they wanted these things to be beautiful, to tell stories with the things they made. Decoration communicates powerful messages, such as spells for protection, and hope embedded in signs and patterns.

M&T: Tell us more about how art connects with the slöjd tradition, and why it's such a vital part of it.

JS: I would say it's about form following function. The knowledge of how to make common, functional items was always a big part of everyday life. They knew, for example, how thick to make a table so that it would be strong, how big that sliding dovetail had to be to make a stable joint. That knowledge of proportions – dimensions, thicknesses, and joinery – is part of the tradition, and is very practical. But when they made things that were connected to certain traditions, like the love gift of a spinning wheel, they made it extraordinarily delicate, with patterns and symbols, and painted it and gave it an ornately carved distaff. It had function in two ways – it was both useful and beautiful. It was meant to show their skills, so the woman receiving the gift would say, "You must be really 'not uncrafty!'" So, there's a union between form and function that connects to folk art.

That's why I tell people I'm not an artist – I'm a craftsman, a *slöjder*. Slöjd is in my roots and my deepest inspiration. I've heard that people want to pay you more if you call yourself an artist, that art is worth more than craft. But slöjd has turned me into who I am – it is folk art and function together, and so I'll never betray my origin and call myself an artist.

M&T: Do you try to balance innovation with tradition? Can you make something new from within those four walls?

JS: Some people think tradition means, "Do it like this, do it like that," – and that approach is very limiting. Slöjd tradition is about freedom. Of course, an object had to be well-built, with good material and strong joints, but aside from that the craftsman was completely free – he had to be, because in the process of making something there is always a personal interaction with the material and the task. No one else can judge your choices. Once the tools, materials, and techniques are learned, the work will come out in an individual way. If my father had said, "This is how a spoon should be, this is how a dough bowl should be," I would have never gotten into it. But what he said was, "If you make a dough bowl, you need to make it three times thicker at the end grain than at the sides, and the base has to be this wide to make it work." And anything else goes. As long as I am true to the material, the use of the cutting tools, then the slöjd traditions and folk-art guide me within these four walls. I'm free to do whatever I want. I can express myself.

M&T: How is slöjd relevant to 21st-century society?

JS: I think that people are probably just the same now as they used to be 200 years ago. We still want to try new things, to learn, to be more skilled, to express ourselves, and to show off. With slöjd, we can do all that by being producers and consumers at the same time. There was a philosopher in the 1800s, Friedrich Engels, who was one of the first to talk about that concept. He warned that the Industrial Revolution was going to cause social problems because the producers would be separate from the consumers and they would be alienated from one another. Instead of connection and unity, there would be anxiety and isolation. You work to earn money, and then buy something you need – but you

Continued on page 16

Chair from Denmark. Courtesy of Jögge Sundqvist.

Flat distaff from Västerbotten. Courtesy of Jögge Sundqvist.

Betida Ludens – The Playing Birch - Photo: Jostein Skeidsvoll

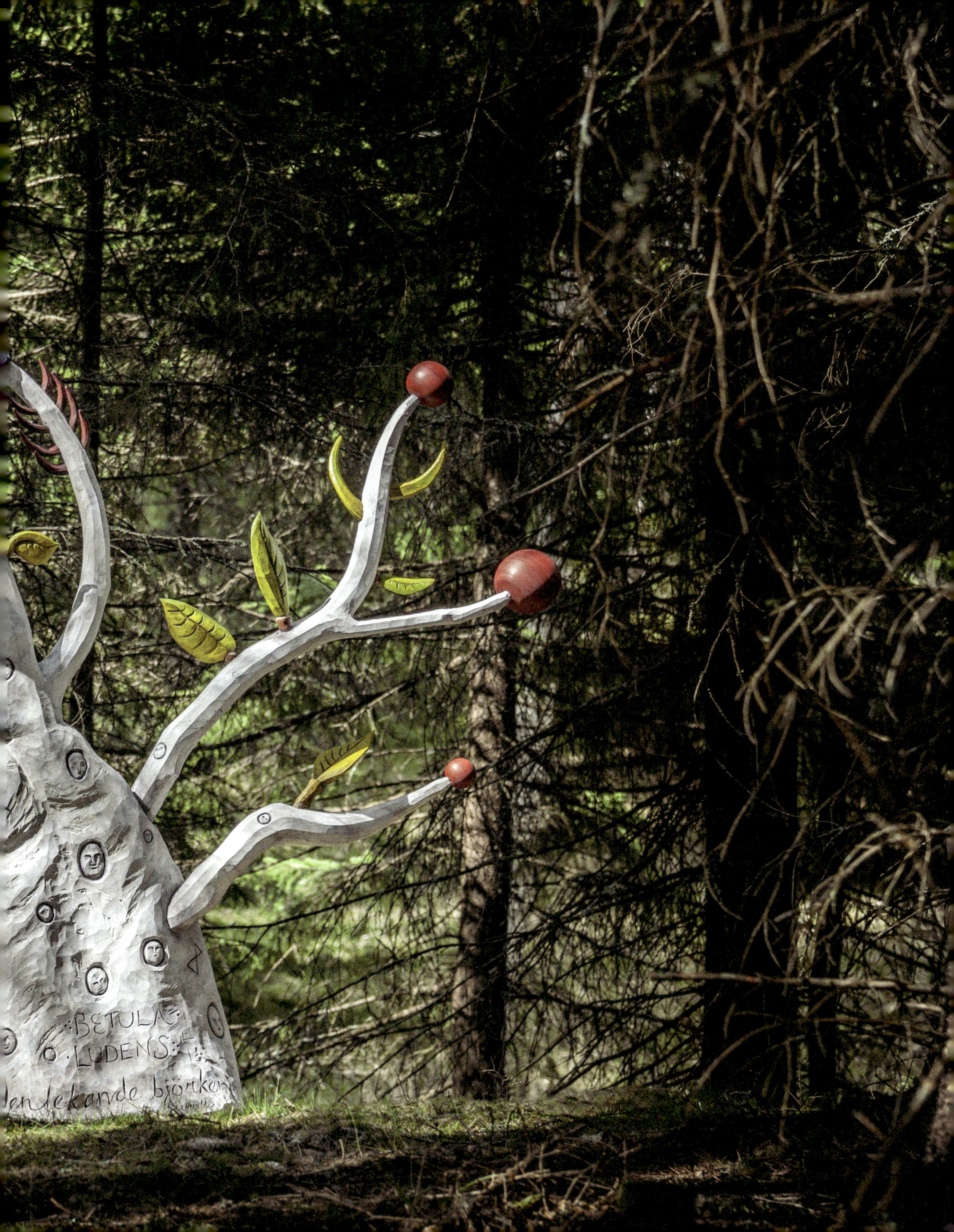
BETULA
LUDENS
lekande björken

Saddle. Naturally bent birch. Västerbotten. Courtesy of Jögge Sundqvist.

don't know what you're getting because you don't know how it is made or how long it's going to last. Your money gives you the option to save time, but when you buy something and it breaks down, you can't fix it. When you're passive and dependent on manufactured items, you feel uneasy about your ability to sustain your standard of living. I'm obviously putting it in stark black and white, but the craftsman who makes a table knows that if a wedge is a little loose, he can take it out and, with his knife, fix it.

  In this era of constant consumerism, slöjd is a survival kit. When I see a person get the spark to do crafts, how they feel more confident with themselves and their skills, and how they can master their environment, it motivates me. If they feel confident in themselves, they'll be a better person to their friends, a good parent to their children – they'll feel like, "I can fix things. I'm not unhandy."

  It seems that being practical has little respect in modern society since we've turned our focus to science and academic credentials. I love science, but I want practical knowledge to be valued equally. Exploring materials, reading fibers, testing moisture content sounds scientific, but using traditional slöjd knowledge, we can use our fingers to do the same thing. Craft is richer because it contains both an intellectual understanding and an intuitive, ingenious working knowledge. The competent craftsperson should be equal to a professor in philosophy – both disciplines are rich, deep, and complex. But society doesn't work that way today – practical work is really undervalued. That is why building an intellectual understanding of slöjd is so important – understanding both the work and the structures behind it. I might be carving a spoon, but it's much more than a spoon. There are the fibers of the wood, how to hold the knife to carve, the long tradition behind the design, the folk art – there is a lot going on that adds value to the work.

  For 35 years, I've been studying in museums and old warehouses, trying to learn how these wooden objects were made. I photographed, took measurements, made notes, and now I think of these things as old woodworking friends. Colleagues. For example, on a naturally bent horse saddle made out of birch in 1775, a man named Johan Johansson made some chip carving. He lived in the county of Västerbotten. I can truly connect to that guy, he's a friend of mine, we work the same way. It's a rich connection.

M&T: Do you believe that slöjd is compatible with modern technology?

JS: The way I see it, machines kill design – they make everything square and perfect because that's what they are designed to do for mass production. It's easy to cut wood on a table saw, plane it on a jointer so it's perfectly 90°, and glue it together. It's a fast way of doing woodwork but it also very clearly affects the overall design. If you do that, you don't get to know the board and you won't learn the subtle things about good material. You won't learn how to look at three-dimensional forms in the way that only working with an axe allows. You'll never be able to find the crook in the tree and the spoon that is in there. Always making straight things is boring, but slöjd enables your designs to evolve.

The Orange Hugger. Photo: Jostein Skeidsvoll.

    Sometimes I use a cordless power drill – I think they're efficient and make the work quick. But this electrical tool never changes my design. When I'm using it, I'm still in control of the angles, and I'm the one who makes all the decisions. As soon as machines start to affect your mindset, so that you go with another design – to change things because the machine tells you it's easier to do it that way – then you're totally lost.

    To use hand tools, you must learn the material and all the techniques of dealing with that material. If you don't understand this, it's so easy to just use power tools, because it seems so fast and efficient. But you'd be missing the whole party – you'd miss the fun part of making the decisions, finding the right material and working with it. When the material talks back to you, suddenly that chair doesn't look the way you were drawing it on paper. You must collaborate with the materials, and that gives so much more joy. And, it is a good feeling to sweat! Yes, it's a creative process, and that's where I want to be as a person.

    Slöjd is about living a good life – a good and creative life that connects me to my history and traditions. I'm trying to take the good sides of the tradition, taking the opportunity to craft my own everyday things the way I want them. Each time I use them, they tell me who I was when I made them, or for whom I was making them, or why – like a memento. It gives me the feeling of being able to shape my own everyday life. Still, I'm a modern man – I still use the internet and electricity. I realize that the old times were a lot of hard work, and I don't want to wear my body out too quickly. I want to take the good parts of tradition as an alternative way to live in a consumer society. By making objects and using them in my everyday life, I'm a producer and I'm a consumer at the same time, which gives me a sense of wholeness.

M&T: How can practicing handcraft give a person a "sense of wholeness?"

JS: This is a hard and very existential question. When people take a class to make spoons, they think it's such a basic thing – a little carving and then hollow the bowl. But there's so much more to it. I want them to feel confident when they do the work, to have fun, to love the way the axe works when they begin to develop control. All of a sudden, they get hooked, and want to practice and improve. This is the fun part – training to get better and better. And it doesn't have to stop – it hasn't stopped for me in 35 years! I still long to do the next one just a little better.

That kind of work gives our lives meaning – we want to explore, to evolve, to find new ways in life and have fun in the journey. I have some friends who hate new stuff – they want to make exactly that same dough bowl 100 times, don't want to change a thing, be super traditional. We need guys like that, too, because they are preserving tradition. We need those who are conservative, and I would say that we also need people who push the boundaries a little and explore. We need all kinds of different people with different attitudes about the craft.

Slöjd makes my body strong, gives me a strong back and muscles – slöjd contains a rich diet for both body and mind. Also, I'm able to repair things when they break. That's why I think of it as a survival kit – in a society where we're trying to be sustainable and live more simply, craft can be a part of that restoration. When we make things, we want to take care of them – we're not throwing them away after five years and buying a new one. This gives you a definition of what quality is. The urge for quality is also an urge for quality of life, where making and beauty give meaning to what a good life is all about. When we don't have to buy so much stuff, we don't use up natural resources and so we make our lives a little bit better. I'm not saying that slöjd is going to change the world, but for me, it's about a transition to a smaller-scale economy.

People sometimes talk about the mindfulness of slöjd, "slöjd meditation," almost like it's a kind of yoga. I think, "Come on, I'm just making spoons!" But I do know what they're talking about. When I have 20 spoons all dry and ready for finish cuts and carving patterns, I have to sit down for eight hours and focus on my work and calm down. After an hour, I'm slowing down and thinking about my family, my ma and pa, my brothers, my daughter and son, my friends, and it feels really good. I can think through problems and find solutions because I can connect to myself when I work with my hands. There has to be a connection between hands-on and mind-on!

M&T: Tell us about your process of making. Are any two objects ever the same?

JS: They can be to a degree, but I love to give them a slight difference. For example, when I make butter knives in batches of 20 or 30, I use a paper template to make each outline. But when I shave them down, they always come out slightly different because of small variations in the material. I have to make a decision on each one – is this going to taper a little more here or there? I can't produce exactly the same thing every time – although it is possible do that working by hand, but what's the point? My aim is to be in the designing process all the time. At a certain point you can say that it's good, it's done, there's nothing more to do. You get feedback from the objects, "Thank you, I'm happy now. Sell me because I am finished."

On the one hand, what I'm doing is mass production, and on the other, each is a unique object. Production is about repetition, and after awhile you stop thinking about the techniques, knife grips, and what you're doing, and you just do it. You get fast and begin to work quickly, and you can focus on design and function, adapting and changing as you go in response to the material.

I make a lot of different objects, from butter knives to big commissions for communities or airports, and materials are always very important. The fun part of hunting for materials is reading the trees, because every tree is different and you can't always tell at first glance what's going on. You have to touch it a little and look, and all of a sudden you can see

Living Out of the Clear Space.

the spoon – the tree talks back to you. It's a kind of interaction with the tree that helps me to find a special form in there. When I'm out spoon hunting I see curves, and filter out everything else. It's like searching the forest for mushrooms – you start to ignore the surroundings and only see the mushrooms.

Finding those crooks is important for my work. In my barn, I have a big room with boxes of different kinds of crooks. When I'm working on a commission for a chair, I pick out different curves to compose it – that's lovely. One commission I had was from The Nordic Museum, the biggest museum in Stockholm. They wanted me to make them a big loveseat – a two-seated chair, in which the back curves like an "s" so that people can sit on opposite sides and talk to each other without touching. I had to tell them that I didn't know if I could do it because I didn't have the tree needed to form that complex bend. So, I went hunting for this special tree, going away early in the morning when the snow's crust was hard. After a day of searching, I hadn't found anything and I almost gave up. But on the second day I saw something in the distance, and I started to walk toward it on the thin crust of the snow. Focusing on that one birch, I could feel it getting wider in my sights as I got closer and the shape became clearer. Suddenly, it was in front of me, and I started to study it. It was good, no knots, no twisting, it was perfect. I heard myself saying, "Do you want to be the back of a loveseat?" It was crazy, but I heard it say, "You want to take me to Stockholm? I've always wanted that! I'm rooted, and you people can travel. Thank you. Cut me down, please!" So, I was happy.

M&T: Your father, Wille, was one of the pioneers of the revival of slöjd, both in the U.S. and in Europe. How did this come about? How does his legacy continue to steer your work?

JS: When he was born in 1925, society was completely different. There were lots of kids where he grew up, and they all had to help with the work of the farm. He had to work in the forest by cutting down trees and taking them home with a sledge and horse, one at a time. The knowledge that he gained was so good, so rich, and firmly rooted in a self-sufficient society.

The Vein of the Tree. Photos: Jostein Skeidsvoll.

This family story is funny and I only understood the depth of it when I became older. When my father was 12 years old, he wanted to draw. He was drawing horses, but he thought his drawings were ugly – the head was much bigger than the body, the legs were too long. One morning out in the forest, he was riding behind the horse in the sledge loaded with some trees he and his father, Arvid, had cut. He described how he found the horse so beautiful, so powerful, and he really wanted to draw it to capture the feeling on paper. So, he got the courage to ask his father if he could take a drawing correspondence course in Stockholm. My grandfather answered, "Draw? Why would you draw a horse when you could just carve one?" My father thought it would be very hard to carve a horse, but my grandpa said, "No, no, it's not hard. Just take a piece of wood and take away everything that is not a horse." The first one he made is still in the family. This was my father's start in woodworking – so this is a story about how a three-dimensional sculpture is easier than making a two-dimensional drawing because his father said so. He already knew good materials, had access to the tools, could easily learn those skills, and had tradi-

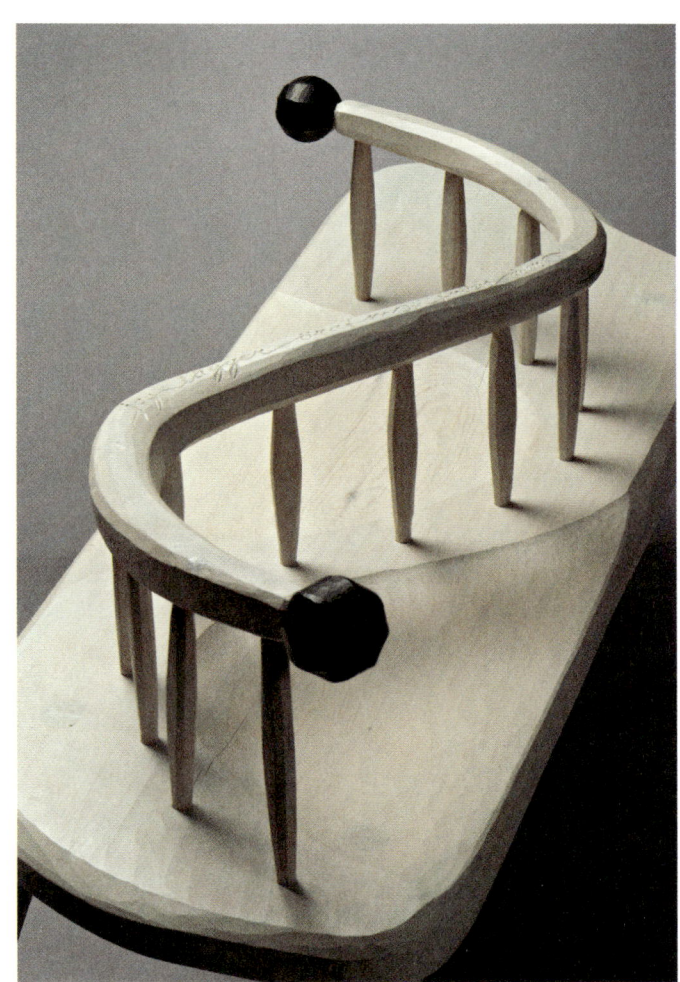

Continued on page 24

Wille Sundqvist. Photo: Jostein Skeidsvoll.

Horse by Wille Sundqvist, age 12. 1938. Willow burl.

Jögge Sundqvist, age 4.

tions to guide him in making three-dimensional objects – it was something done naturally every day. He loved making horses and did it all throughout his life.

When my father was in his 20s, he didn't know what to do – he came from the self-sufficient northern part of the country, and his dialect was hard to understand in the southern part of Sweden. He had grown up on a farm without electricity, and was trying to get assimilated into modern Swedish society. He tried several different jobs and tried to be a gardener, but people were impressed with the way he could use a knife. They said, "You should teach slöjd in the school, you really know the old ways." Suddenly, these skills were valuable, and my father wanted to share them with other people.

He was a good teacher, keen on helping people, showing them not just how to hold their hands when carving, but how to think about process. I eventually picked up that urge to share craft with other people, but when I was 15, I hated it when he told me too much how things should be. I was singing and playing guitar in a rock and roll band, and he was very religious, so there was a disconnect, so to say. When I was a little older, I started to ask him about techniques: "How do you do that knife grip?" We had a very good relationship then. He was such a dedicated carver – even if we had friends at home, we'd be sitting having coffee after dinner and he'd take out some spoons and carve as we talked. We all knew that he could talk much better if he had something in his hands. He would even bring his carving along on trains – he couldn't stop. He was a very gentle, humble man in his work, and led a rich life as a craftsman.

M&T: Your father has used a quote from the Faroe Islands that "a knifeless man is a lifeless man." In a similar vein, it seems you see slöjd as a way to develop self-reliance and joy in life. Is that a fair summary?

JS: Yes, and this expression is used in Sweden, too. When I grew up, everyone had a knife on their belt. In everyday life, opening packages, cutting a piece of wire, you needed a knife. When you didn't have it, you felt naked. It was a part of everyday life, and almost everything you used was made of wood. When you had a problem and something needed repair, you took out your knife and fixed it. Well, I try to work in line with my belief that craft is good for people. Of course, you need to tighten your belt as a craftsman, but life is so much more than money in the bank and a high material standard of living. Satisfaction and self-confidence come to me with my ability to shape the things that surround me, and I want to share it with others. I want to make objects that are both sculptural and functional. I work within these four walls because that's where I'm rooted, where I'm happy to be. I also like to travel, to see other countries, because I love to spread the word about craft. When I see the joy and happiness that comes from learning, it makes me happy. I want to share that. ◆

Bench. *Kitty Hawk 1904*. Pine. Naturally bent birch. Photo: Jostein Skeidsvoll.

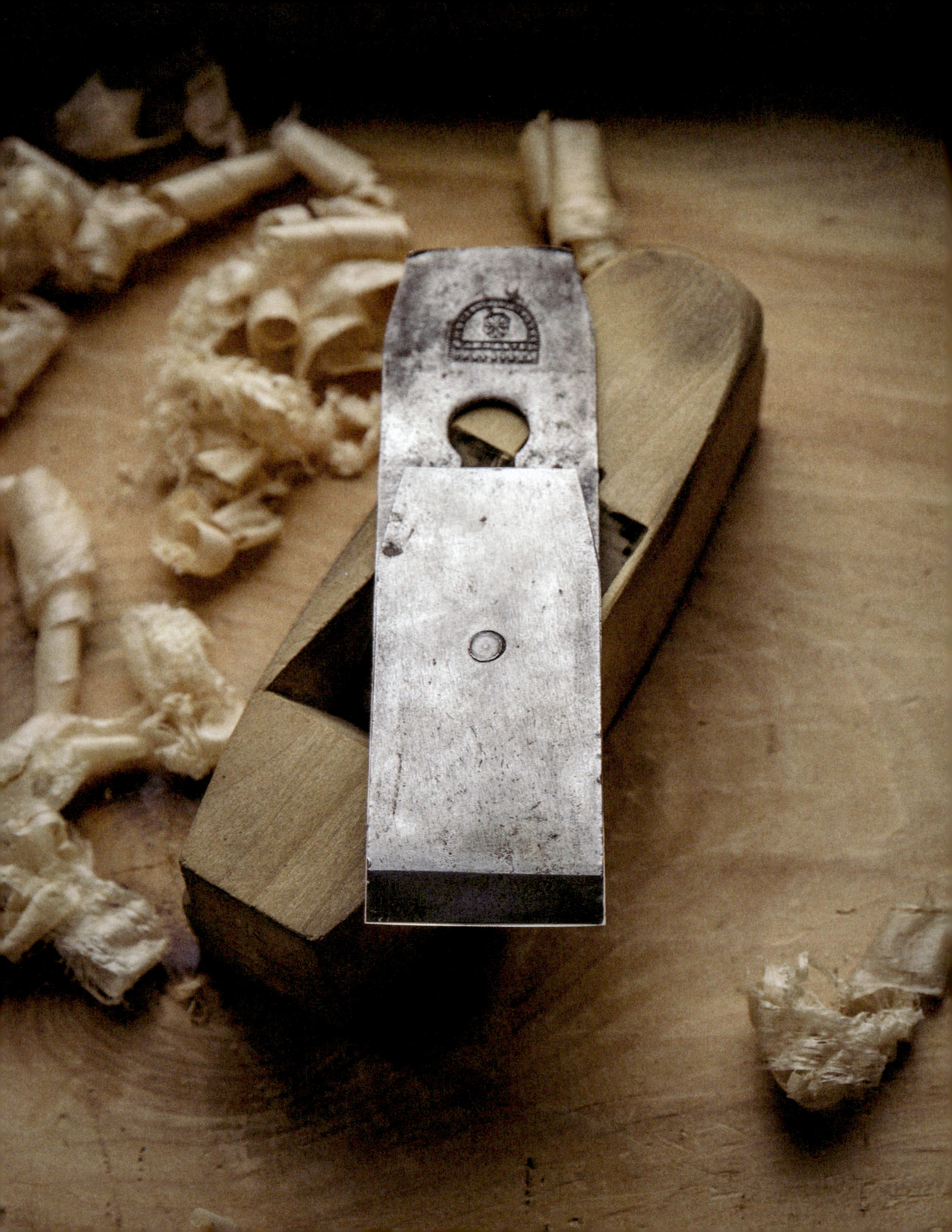

CUTTING-EDGE TECHNOLOGY
Rediscovering the Double-iron Plane

STEVE VOIGT

In the early 1990s, I began my woodworking journey with a couple of vintage Stanley bench planes and a *Fine Woodworking* book on hand tools. I dutifully followed the book's instructions on setting up and sharpening my new planes, and everything was going pretty well until I came to the section on setting the cap iron (also known as the chipbreaker). According to the author, for difficult hardwoods I was supposed to set the edge of the cap iron "as close as possible" to the cutting edge. So I did, and disaster ensued. I could barely push the plane; it shuddered, shook, and quickly came to an unceremonious halt, the mouth hopelessly clogged with balled-up shavings. I moved the cap iron to a safe distance (about 1/16" - 1/8") from the cutting edge, and there it would stay for nearly two decades.

After that initial experience, I readily embraced the late 20th-century conventional wisdom that cap irons were a con game foisted on a gullible public, and that their real purpose was to make the planemaker's job easier, and perhaps to stiffen the cutting iron, allowing for the use of thinner, cheaper irons. If you wanted to stop tear-out, forget the cap iron: You needed a single-iron plane with a tight mouth, a thick iron, and a high cutting angle of 55° or higher. The ubiquitous Stanley/Bailey plane with a cap iron, otherwise known as a double-iron plane, was for rough carpentry, not fine furniture. And the instructions I had read in that *Fine Woodworking* book, along with similar instructions in texts dating back nearly 200 years, were just plain wrong.

In 2012, I began to see discussions about cap irons popping up on the internet. Spurred by a Japanese film of a cap iron on a planing machine, a number of woodworkers taught themselves to use the cap iron the way it had been described in all those earlier sources. The results they obtained, and in some cases documented, were dramatic, and by following their detailed descriptions, I was soon able to achieve equally spectacular results. The double iron stopped tear-out more effectively than any other method, required less physical effort, and left a better surface finish. Those old texts weren't wrong; they just weren't detailed enough. The double iron is a finicky instrument, and if it's not set up just right, it won't work at anywhere near its tremendous potential.

Though thrilled with my newfound success, I felt a nagging uneasiness. How could I have been so wrong? And more important, how could the purveyors of the conventional wisdom about cap irons – planemakers, hand-tool gurus, professional woodworkers – have been so wrong as well?

The search for answers led me in two directions. One was to become the first commercial U.S. maker in nearly a century of traditional British/American wooden double-iron planes. But that is a story for another time. The other direction was a deep dive into the history of the double iron, dating back over 250 years. And what I found was an amazing story. In the late 18th century, the double iron was a revolutionary, disruptive technology. In a relatively short period of time, it dominated the market for bench planes, so that by the late 19th century, one respected author would note that "as…planes are made with both double and single irons, it should be said that the latter, though cheaper, are not suitable for cabinet working."

But perhaps I should start at the beginning…

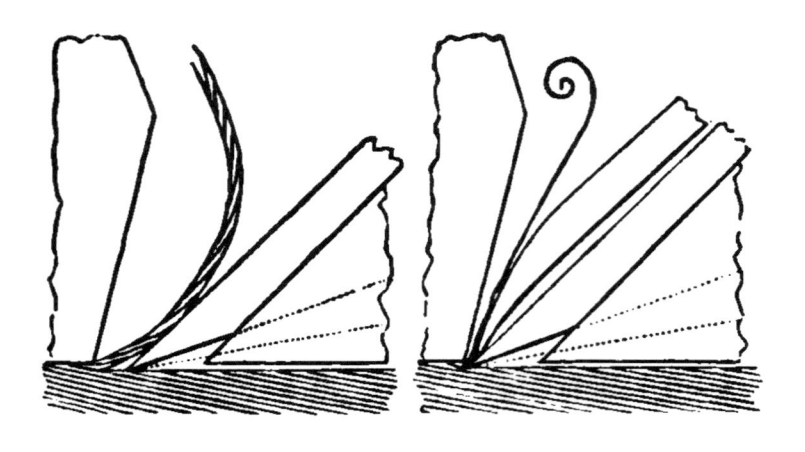

"[The single-iron plane at far left shows] the shaving is more suddenly bent in passing its narrower mouth, so that the cutting now begins to exceed the splitting, as the wood is held down by the closer mouth: the shaving is more broken and polygonal, but the work is left smoother.

"The same effects are obtained in a much superior manner in the planes with double irons, such as in [the right image], the top iron is not intended to cut, but to present a more nearly perpendicular wall for the ascent of the shavings, the top iron more effectually breaks the shavings, and is thence sometimes called the break iron.

"Now therefore, the shaving being very thin, and constrained between two approximate edges, it is as it were bent out of the way to make room for the cutting edge, so that the shaving is removed by absolute cutting, and without being in any degree split or rent off."

– Charles Holtzapffel, 1846

Development of the Cap Iron

Prior to the invention of the double iron, the main method for combating the problem of tear-out with handplanes was to increase the bed angle of the plane: The higher the angle, the less the tear-out. While few bench planes before 1750 survive, there is evidence that planemakers in the 17th and early 18th centuries offered them in a variety of pitches: common pitch (45° or 47.5°) for softwoods and tasks such as house joinery, and higher pitches for hardwoods and cabinetry.[1] But in the late 18th century, double-iron planes supplanted high-pitched single-iron bench planes, though the higher pitches continued to be used for molding and joinery planes.

The origins of the double iron are somewhat mysterious, but probably date to the mid-18th century. A double-iron smoothing plane discovered in London during an archaeological dig may have been made as early as 1750.[2] The most interesting feature of this plane is that while the business end of the cap iron is typical, there is no mechanism for fastening the cap iron to the cutting iron. The two irons are loose, held together by the wedge, so the owner would have to set both irons by tapping them independently. This arrangement supports the theory that the earliest double iron was simply two cutting irons that some enterprising craftsman placed back-to-back.

The first written reference to the double iron dates to 1767. In an advertisement in a Pennsylvania newspaper,[3] Samuel Carruthers offered planes for sale, including "double-iron'd planes, of a late construction, far exceeding any tooth planes or uprights whatsoever, for cross grained or curled stuff." Translation: double-iron planes, recently invented, perform far better than toothing planes or high-angle planes in wood with difficult grain.[4]

It's tempting to write off Carruthers' claims as mere advertising hyperbole, but more impartial sources from the 18th century back him up. One of the earliest is Salivet's *Manuel du Tourneur* (1792). After a basic description of the double iron, Salivet writes that the cutting iron, when bedded at the normal angle, "would tear out a lot if the shavings were to enter the throat at that angle. The bevel of the top iron, lifts the shaving and forces it from the inclination at which it was started. But the two irons must not be even; the bottom one should be a little bit ahead. The less the difference, the less tear-out produced, to the point where one can plane oak branches, even almost green ones; this is the most difficult test that can be done."

Here we have perhaps the first description of how the cap iron works, and how to use it. The cap iron forces the shaving to bend, which prevents the wood from splitting ahead of the cut, thus reducing tear-out. And the closer the cutting edge is to the cap iron, the more effectively it will work.

Salivet's description is fleshed out in greater detail in Peter Nicholson's *The Mechanic's Companion*, which, along with André Roubo's *L'art du Menuisier*, is one of the most important first-person accounts of 18th-century woodworking. Nicholson's book was first published (under another title) in 1812, but reflects the author's experience as an apprentice and cabinetmaker in the 1780s. Nicholson's description of the double iron begins:

> To prevent the iron from tearing the wood to cross-grained stuff [stock], a cover is used with a reversed basil [bevel], and fastened by means of a screw.

Nicholson, like Carruthers and Salivet, is claiming that the cap iron will prevent tear-out in wood with cranky grain. He continues:

> The basil of the cover must be rounded, and not flat, as that of the iron is. The distance between the cutting edge of the iron, and the edge of the cover, depends altogether on the nature of the stuff. If the stuff is free, the edge of the cover may be set at a considerable distance, because the difficulty of pushing the plane forward becomes greater, as the edge of the cover is nearer the edge of the iron, and the contrary when more remote.

In the first sentence, Nicholson explains that the bevel of the cap iron must be curved, unlike the flat bevel of the cutting iron (we'll look at why this is necessary a bit later). He then explains the proportional relationship between the difficulty of the wood being planed and the setting of the cap iron: When the wood is straight-grained, the cap iron can be "set at a considerable distance" from the cutting edge, but when the grain is curly or reversing, the cap iron must be closer to the edge. However, the closer the cap iron gets, the more difficult it is to push the plane, because of the force required to deflect the shaving at the point of the cut.

In the glossary of *The Mechanic's Companion*, Nicholson adds one more note on the double iron:

> The double iron planes now in use, are a most complete remedy against cross-grained and curling stuff; the plane will nearly work as smooth against the grain as with it.

It's clear from Salivet's and Nicholson's writings that by the late 18th century, the effectiveness of the cap iron and the mechanics of its function were well understood. What's also clear is that consumers of that era enthusiastically embraced double-iron planes, and were willing to pay a steep premium for them. In 1786, planemaker Thomas Napier published a price list of more than 50 planes in the Philadelphia *Freeman's Journal*.[5] Napier offered all the common bench planes with single or double irons (excepting the fore plane, which was offered only with single iron). A double-iron smoothing plane from Napier cost 9 shillings, more than twice the price of a single-iron smoother, which sold for a mere 4 shillings. A double-iron jointer cost 15 shillings, a 34-percent premium over a single-iron jointer (11 shillings, 3 pence). Napier, unlike Carruthers, offers no comment on the characteristics of double irons – presumably the novelty had worn off – but the price differential suggests that the superior quality of the double iron was by now an accepted fact.

In 1797, Joseph Seaton purchased a complete set of cabinetmaker's tools for his son, Benjamin, who crafted the famous "Seaton Tool Chest" to hold the tools. Seaton's inventory shows that of the seven bench planes originally contained in the chest, five were double iron; only a smoother and a jack plane were single iron.[6] It seems that by the close of the 18th century, the double iron had established a dominant position in the marketplace.

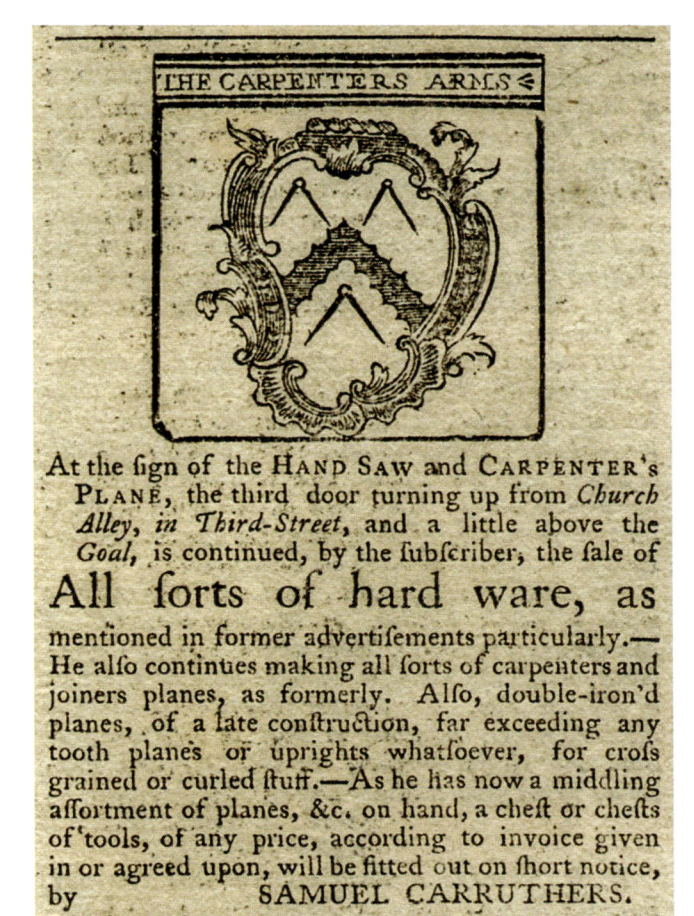

Obsolescence of the High-pitched Bench Plane

The arrival of price lists and illustrated catalogs of woodworking tools in the 19th century was an important development, which gives us detailed information about what tools were available. Studying these catalogs, one finds plenty of common pitch single-iron planes (though always at a lower price than double-iron planes), but no mention of higher angles. As I noted previously, early planemakers offered bench planes in a variety of pitches, but as soon as the double iron became available, the high-pitched single-iron planes disappeared. It's worth speculating about why this happened, especially considering that high angles continued to be used for molding planes, where a cap iron is not usually a practical option.

I believe there are several reasons the high-pitched option became obsolete. First, pushing a high-angle plane takes a lot more effort. While a closely set cap iron, as Nicholson noted, also increases the force required to push the plane, a significant advantage of the cap iron is that it can be adjusted to the task at hand: When the wood is straight grained, the cap iron can be moved back, reducing the force needed; only when the grain becomes difficult is the closer setting needed.

A consequence of the increased resistance of high angles is the need to use narrower irons and lighter cuts. I know of no modern maker of high-angle planes who offers an iron wider than 2-1/4", but in the double-iron era, irons of up to 2-3/4" in width were common. And even with a 2-1/4" iron, it's pretty difficult to push a high-angle plane through anything more than a light cut.

An additional concern is the mouth. High-pitched planes often need a tight mouth; the high angle alone is not enough to stop tear-out in adverse circumstances. But a tight mouth is the Achilles heel of wooden planes: If it's tight enough to stop tear-out, it prevents the user from taking anything but the thinnest shavings. Furthermore, wooden planes require regular flattening of the sole, and each time the sole is flattened, the mouth opens a little; it is not long before the mouth opening is too wide to have any effect on tear-out. A double-iron plane, on the other hand, doesn't need a tight mouth; the cap iron alone controls tear-out.

A final factor is the life of the cutting edge. The higher the plane's pitch, the more quickly the cutting edge will wear out, as anyone who has used a scraper can attest. The simple high-carbon tool steels in use at the time, though easy to sharpen, are less wear-resistant than most of the tool steels in use today, so edge retention would have been a real issue. Of interest, a fellow planemaker recently told me that while he likes using vintage cutting irons in his double-iron planes, he only uses O1 steel for his high-pitched planes.

Woodworkers in the pre-industrial era worked entirely by hand, and flattening and thicknessing lumber had to be done quickly and efficiently. Workers needed planes that could take wide, heavy cuts and go a long time between sharpening, yet they still needed to control tear-out. Given this, it's easy to see why high-pitched planes fell out of favor.

Another important development in the 19th century is the appearance of self-instruction manuals for woodworking (and other trades). Roubo and Nicholson were like cultural anthropologists, describing the workings of the various trades for posterity, but later in the 19th century we start to see books aimed specifically at amateurs who want to learn a hobby. Unsurprisingly, the authors of these woodworking texts continued to describe the use of the double iron, and to stress its superiority over single irons. James Lukin, in *Our Workshop: Being a Practical Guide to the Amateur in the Art of Carpentry and Joinery* (1879), using the term "break iron" instead of cap iron, writes:

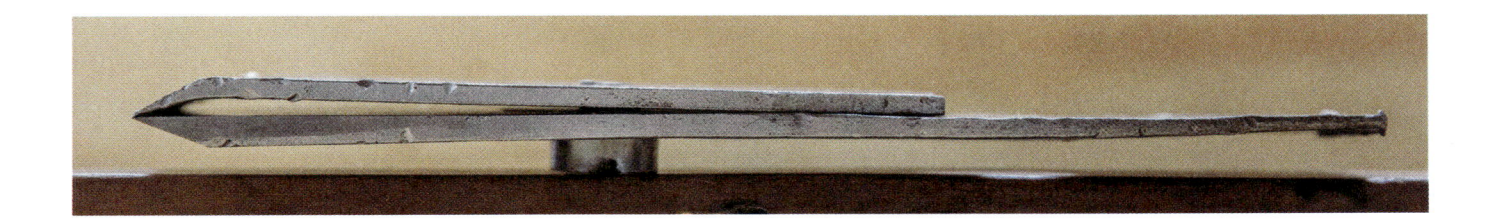

> The break iron of the jack plane is generally fixed, so that its edge…is one-sixteenth behind the edge of the cutter. If the break iron be set back, say one-eighth of an inch, it will not bend the shavings sufficiently, and the planing will very probably be rough. The nearer the edges of the irons are to each other…the smoother will be the work produced, but the labour of driving the plane will be much increased.…Planes having single irons are much less laborious to handle, but the work executed by them is neither so smooth nor so truthful as that of the double-ironed description. The shavings escape in long curls or ribands from a single iron, and the surface of the work is left somewhat rough. It is a good plan to remove the first exterior and dirt from a plank with a single-ironed plane, after which the jack and smoothing planes will work pleasantly, and retain their edges for a longer time.

Similarly, David Denning in *The Art and Craft of Cabinet-Making* (1891) explains the advantage of the double iron as follows:

> In any double iron plane, the nearer the two edges are together the finer will be the shaving, but the labour of planing will be increased. From this it will be seen that the relative positions of the two irons is of considerable importance, and that within certain limits, the planes can be regulated to suit the work on hand. As jack, trying, and smoothing planes are made with both double and single irons, it should be said that the latter, though cheaper, are not suitable for cabinet work.

In the first half of the 20th century, the wooden bench plane became an endangered species, replaced almost entirely by the ubiquitous Stanley/Bailey plane and its imitators. Interestingly, this further cemented the dominance of the double iron. Throughout the 19th century, wooden planemakers had offered single-iron planes as a cheaper option, but after 1926, when the last U.S. manufacturer of wooden planes closed its doors,[7] a double iron was virtually the only choice for a new bench plane. Meanwhile, woodworking writers continued to sing the praises of the double iron. The prolific Charles Hayward wrote more than a dozen columns on the subject. In a typical example, which by now will sound very familiar to the reader, he writes that the cap iron's purpose is to break the shaving as it is raised, and so minimize any tendency of the grain to tear out. He says that the closer to the edge it is set the more effective it becomes, but the greater the resistance it offers. For the jack plane it can be set about 1/16" from the edge; the trying plane (when set fine) about 1/32", the smoothing plane 1/32" or less.[8]

Decline & Resurgence

Hayward's writing is suffused with a poignant awareness that the 20th century was a time of inexorable decline in the use and manufacture of hand tools. All sorts of skills and techniques that were taken for granted in previous centuries disappeared, and the use of the double iron wasn't immune from this trend. By the end of the 20th century it was common, as I noted earlier, to hear the claim that cap irons didn't really stop tear-out. Some writers speculated that the real purpose of the cap iron was to stabilize or add heft to the cutting iron. One prominent author wrote that cap irons "do more harm than good in a handplane" – a statement that would have shocked any late 18th-century woodworker. But it wasn't just teachers and writers: Planemakers clearly didn't understand the double iron either.

The common denominator in planemaking at the end of the 20th century was a search for any solution to the problem of tear-out that didn't involve the double iron. A few makers began offering traditional wooden bench planes, but only in a high-angle, single-iron format. Infill planemakers also emphasized high angles, often combined with extremely tight mouths. Metal plane manufacturers made bevel-up planes (which can use high cutting angles and don't have cap irons) and high-angle frogs (which allowed users of bevel-down planes to have 50° or 55° cutting angles).

In addition, a number of companies marketed "improved" cap irons that were purported to be better than the Stanley/Bailey cap iron, a claim based solely on the fact that they were made of thicker steel. The problem is, they don't actually do what a cap iron was designed to do: stop tear-out. In this respect, the original Leonard Bailey design is far better than the "improved" version. Bailey clearly understood how a cap iron functioned, while his modern counterparts did not. And the vast majority of users who purchased new planes didn't notice: No one had taught them to use the cap iron correctly. The device that had revolutionized woodworking more than two centuries earlier had become an appendage, seemingly useless, its original purpose and function virtually forgotten.

But if the 20th century was marked by the disappearance of many traditional skills, the early 21st century has seen at least the partial recovery of those skills. The impetus for the revival of the double iron came not from historical texts, but from a film made by Chutaro Kato and Yasunori Kawai, professors at Yamagata University in Japan.[9] The slow-motion, highly magnified images show how effective the cap iron can be. In addition, the film quantifies the distances at which the cap iron is effective (roughly .004"-.012") and the angle on the leading edge of the cap iron (somewhere between 50° and 80°). The film had actually been around for years, but the addition of English subtitles by Mia Iwasaki in 2012 made it comprehensible and accessible to many more woodworkers. I was one of many woodworkers who, after seeing the video and reading online discussions, began to experiment with the cap iron, and the results were a revelation in two ways. First, as I've said already, the double iron, once it was properly set up, worked spectacularly. Nasty exotic hardwoods; swirling, reversing grain; knots; quartersawn surfaces – all of these and more succumbed to the double iron.

The bigger revelation, though, was that those 18th- and 19th-century sources had been right all along. When Nicholson wrote, more than 200 years ago, that a double-iron plane "will nearly work as smooth against the grain as with it," he wasn't kidding, and neither were the many others who extolled the benefits of the double iron from the 18th to the 20th centuries. All the convoluted strategies for combating tear-out that had been tried in the late 20th century turned out to be unnecessary – the solution was sitting under everyone's noses all along.

In hindsight then, the decline and resurgence of the cap iron is a cautionary tale. It suggests that when evaluating methods of work from past centuries, we should start from the assumption that these earlier practitioners knew what they were doing; we should give them the benefit of the doubt until proven otherwise. And we ought to look skeptically on a lot of 20th-century ideas, especially those that suggest that earlier methods were primitive or inefficient. During my research, I came upon an early 19th-century text in which the author described the double iron in typically effusive language. In this case, though, a late 20th-century editor felt compelled to scold the author, writing that "a fine mouth and a high angle are more important for planing difficult wood than is a double iron....Here we see a contemporary reference that suggests otherwise, but the reference cannot be taken at face value."

The modern editor had it exactly wrong: Taking texts like this one at face value, more or less literally, is exactly what needed to be done. It's easy to assume that we, with our modern technology, are smarter than workers of centuries past, but when it comes to working with our hands, that's probably not the case. I'm fairly confident that there are other traditional technologies like the double iron that have been misunderstood and forgotten, still out there, just waiting to be rediscovered.

Using a Cap Iron

In the last few years, a number of high-quality videos and articles, freely available on the internet, have made learning to use the cap iron easier than ever.[10] I won't regurgitate what those woodworkers have already said, but I'd like to offer some commentary to help novices sort through the process of making the cap iron work.

First, make sure your cap iron has the correct geometry. Cap irons from the 18th and 19th centuries (for wooden planes) have a curved bevel; the angle at

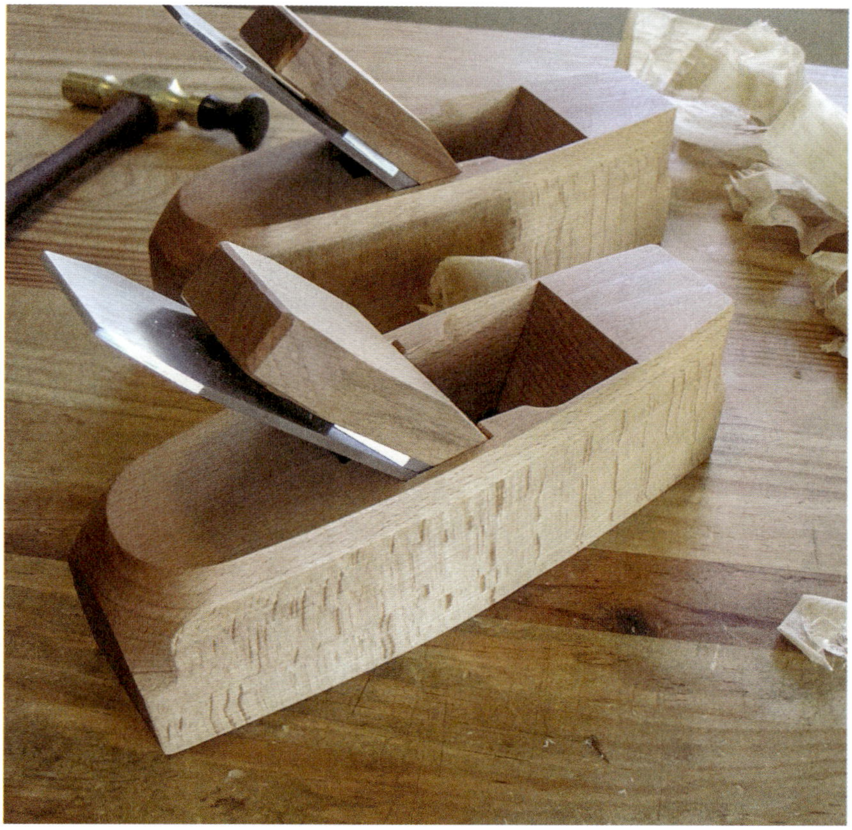

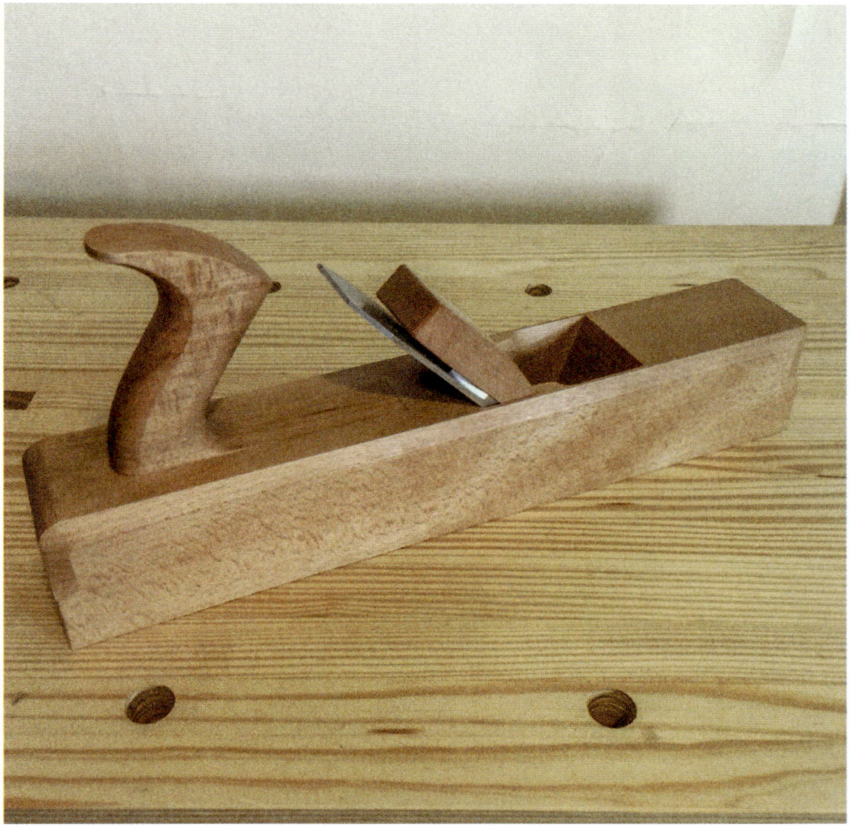

the tip is approximately 45°, but the profile quickly becomes more shallow. Let's consider why this is so.

In 1846, Charles Holtzapffel wrote that the cap iron should "present a more nearly perpendicular wall for the ascent of the shavings."[11] Because the cutting iron of a common-pitch plane is usually bedded at 45°, adding a cap iron with a final angle of approximately 45° gives us the 90° "wall" that Holtzapffel describes. However, if the cap iron simply had a flat 45° bevel, the shavings would be trapped and the plane would clog immediately. The curved shape of the traditional cap iron allows the shavings to be ejected efficiently.

The original cap irons on vintage Stanley/Bailey planes, with their characteristic hump, look quite different than traditional cap irons, but what counts is the geometry at the business end. I have examined a number of old stock Stanley cap irons and found that the angle at the tip always approximates 45°. As I said before, Leonard Bailey clearly knew what he was doing.

So, if you are using an old wooden plane, or a Stanley/Bailey with the original cap iron, you won't need to change the geometry. You do need to make sure that the cap iron is moderately sharp; there should not be a blunt flat at the tip. If there is, hone the cap iron, following the curved shape, until you raise a burr. Then hone the underside of the cap iron – don't use a microbevel, just hone the flat part of the underside – until you flip the burr over; this should ensure a gap-free fit against the cutting iron. Finish by stropping the burr off on a piece of plain leather.

The so-called "improved" cap irons made by modern manufacturers generally have a flat bevel of 25°, far too shallow to break the shavings the way they should. Without modification, these cap irons won't stop tear-out to any significant degree. Fortunately, there is an easy fix: add a small (about 1/64") microbevel to the tip. The exact angle isn't critical; I recommend approximately 50°, but anything from 45° to 60° will work well. The 80° bevel used in the Kato/Kawai video will also work, but most users will find it uncomfortably steep. In general, the steeper the angle, the more rapidly the resistance to planing increases as you move the cap iron closer to the cutting edge.

Once you've got the right geometry, find a test board – something with ugly, but not totally nightmarish grain. Sharpen your iron, set the cap iron well back, and take moderately fine shavings. You should be getting some ugly tear-out; if you're not, get a nastier board. Or flip the board around and plane against the grain. The point is, you'll never know how effective the cap iron is unless you first set up a situation where a sharp iron alone is not enough.

Next, set the cap iron closer. In his video on the subject, Christopher Schwarz shows how to use an automotive feeler gauge for the initial setting. I think this is a great idea. Start with an .008" gauge. As Schwarz says, you'll soon get a feel for the correct distance and you won't need to use the feeler gauges any more. Make sure the mouth is open: About 1/32" is good, but more is fine, too. A lot of old wooden planes have giant mouths; it doesn't matter. The mouth is irrelevant when you have a cap iron.

Finally, plane away. The tear-out should quickly disappear; you should be able to see it lessen, then vanish as you take successive passes. If the tear-out isn't going away, move the cap iron closer to the cutting edge. If the plane is too hard to push, move the cap iron away from the cutting edge. Experiment, observe the results, and experiment some more. A couple of visual clues can help: One clear sign that the cap iron is doing its job is if the shavings shoot straight out of the plane without curling up. If the shavings are curly, the cap iron may not be close enough, or the depth of cut may be too small to allow the cap iron to do its job. On the other hand, if the shavings are bunched up like crinkled bacon, the cap iron may be too close (though in some situations, that degree of closeness is necessary to defeat tear-out, so it's not automatically bad).

People often ask: Will this work with cambered irons? The answer is yes. I do not recommend shaping the cap iron to match the camber of the cutting iron – keep the edge of the cap iron straight. An interesting strategy suggested by Richard Maguire is to set the outer edges of the cap iron flush (or nearly so) with the outer edges of a cambered cutting iron. Thus, on a smoothing plane, which normally has only a tiny bit of camber, the cap iron will be very close; on a trying or jointer plane, with moderate camber, the cap iron will be a bit farther away, and on a jack plane, with heavy camber, the cap iron will be farther still. I find this strategy a bit too rigid to use all the time, but it's a great starting point for working with cambered irons.

As with most woodworking techniques, the use of the cap iron takes some practice to master. But once you've experienced this revolutionary technology for yourself, you'll see why 18th-century woodworkers understood it to be, in Peter Nicholson's words, "a most complete remedy against cross-grained and curling stuff." ◆

ENDNOTES

1. 19th- and 20th-century writers use labels such as "York pitch" (50°), "middle pitch" (55°), and "half pitch" (60°); however, I am not aware of any use of these terms before 1843. The only 18th-century references to high pitch I have seen use the terms "upright" (discussed in note 4) and "half-upright." The precise meanings of these terms are not clear.
2. Chris Green, "An Early Cabinetmaker's Smoothing Plane from the City of London," *Tools and Trades History Society*, accessed 1/30/19. http://taths.org.uk/tools-trades/articles/49-an-early-cabinet-maker-s-smoothing-plane-from-the-city-of-london.
3. *The Pennsylvania Chronicle and Universal Advertiser*, March 2-9, 1767.
4. The term "upright" is not common, but most likely refers to a very high-angle plane (greater than 60°). A photo of what appears to be an early 18th-century jointer plane with a bed angle of approximately 65° is shown in Jeffrey Greene, *American Furniture in the 18th Century* (Newtown, CT: The Taunton Press, Inc., 1996), 118.
5. *The Freeman's Journal: Or, the North-American Intelligencer*, May 31, 1786.
6. Jane Rees and Mark Rees, eds., *The Tool Chest of Benjamin Seaton*, 2nd edition (Essex, UK: Tools And Trades History Society, 2012).
7. The Sandusky Tool Company was the last U.S. maker. From 1926 until I started my planemaking business in 2015, there were no North American commercial makers of traditional wooden double-iron planes.
8. Charles Hayward, ed., *The Woodworker: Charles H. Hayward Years: 1939-1967*, Volume I (Ft. Mitchell, KY: Lost Art Press, 2016), 154.
9. Numerous pirated copies of the video can be found on YouTube; please instead view it at the authorized site: https://vimeo.com/158558759.
10. Christopher Schwarz's "Fine Tune a Handplane's Back Iron" (https://www.popularwoodworking.com/woodworking-blogs/fine-tune-a-hand-planes-back-iron/) is the most clear, succinct explanation I have seen. David Weaver's "Setting a Cap Iron" (http://www.woodcentral.com/articles/test/articles_935.shtml) was the first explanation written in the wake of the Kato/Kawai film, and goes into more detail. Richard Maguire's "Tuning Hand Planes – Setting the Cap Iron/Chipbreaker" (https://www.youtube.com/watch?v=xmDVa5cxq8w) is still more detailed. For these and more suggestions, see the "Links of Interest" section of my website: http://www.voigtplanes.com/links.html.
11. Charles Holtzapffel, *Turning and Mechanical Manipulation, Volume II* (1846; repr., London: Holtzapffel & Co., 1875), 480.

A Chair Called Henry

Nathaniel Brewster

"There is truth to certain forms – those things that stay the same without regard for location or time."

– Elliott Snyder

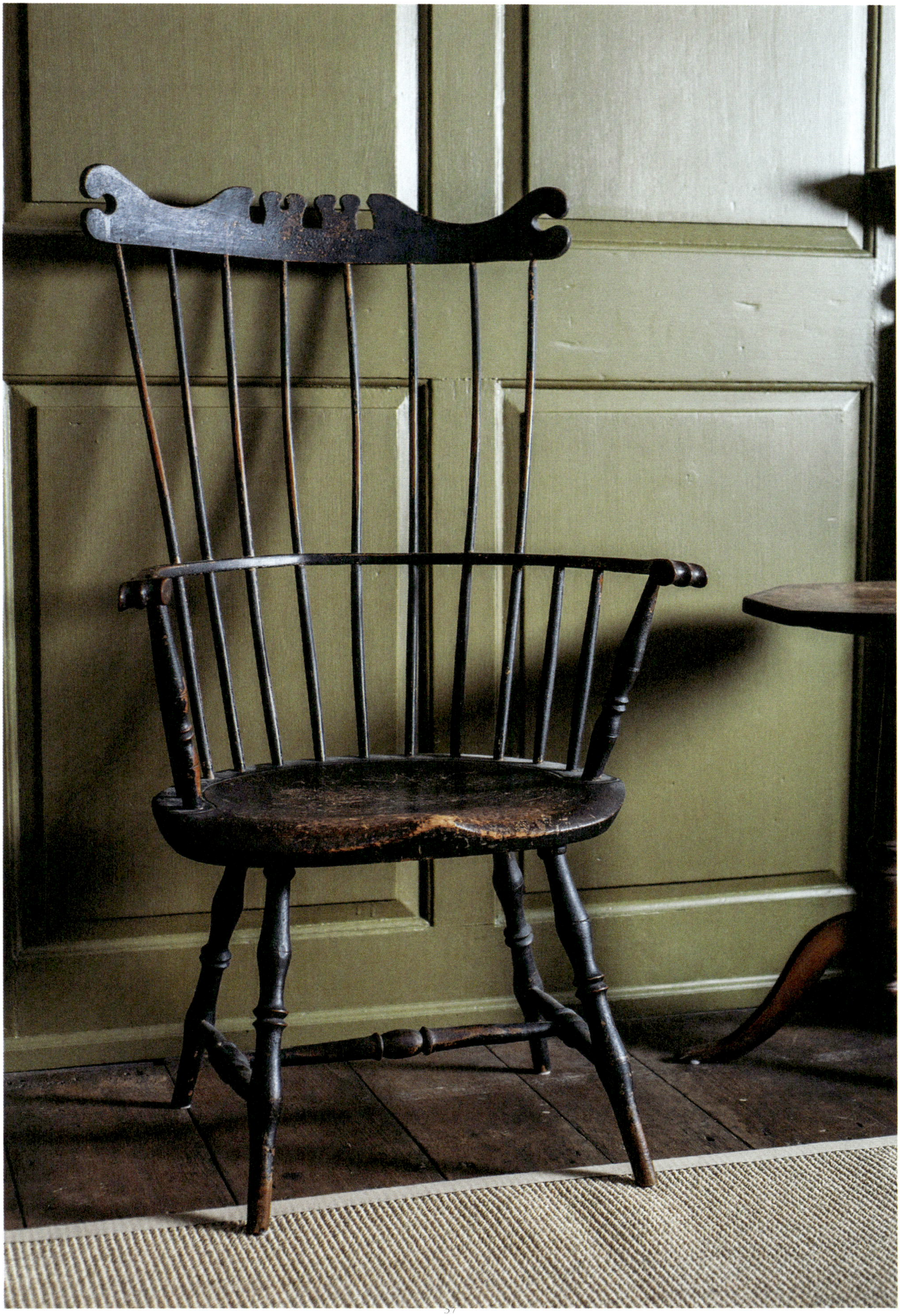

Like so many Windsors, our chair is an anonymous work – a puzzle that spans nearly 250 years and perhaps two states. Thankfully, it has avoided catastrophe over the centuries and remains intact, untouched black paint and all, to serve as something as transcendent as it is enigmatic. There is beauty in that mystery – something captivating in its design and its origin.

In late 2018, this chair was on the market for $30,000. While that might seem like an extraordinary sum – and it is – it remains only a fraction of the value of a similarly uncommon Queen Anne or Chippendale side chair from the same era. In many ways, "country furniture," like our Windsor, is a bargain, even if it is worth more than 30 times other competent examples of the form. Due to a fabled combination of style, substance, and rarity, its value is no mystery – simple market mathematics with a sprinkle of salesmanship and provenance.

But an object this unique is far more than the sum of its sale price. It begs for deeper analysis, and not the sort that can be quantified in angles and inches. The stuff I'm interested in – the stuff that truly makes this chair extraordinary – cannot be duplicated in measured drawings. I'm on the hunt for something more abstract. Why did our 18th-century maker depart so markedly from the design standards of the day? What can this Windsor's form tell us about the community in which it was made? Who, in the 1770s, would own such a rambunctious piece of furniture? And what should we do with it now?

The Collectors

My journey began in the summer of 2018 at the western Massachusetts home of collectors and dealers Elliott and Grace Snyder. It was hot, and the leaves of the New England hardwoods were at their greenest. The Snyders came to collecting together, both in their twenties and fresh out of graduate school, with an empty old house in need of the necessities. It was a small 18th-century place in Lebanon, Connecticut, near the famed Lebanon Green, that, as both note, "would have looked terrible with modern furniture."[1] Even then, in the late 1960s, the two had a love of history and a taste for country antiques. Their journey from young academics to noted collectors and dealers spans over 40 years. From their historic house in Lebanon, to a Dutch stone house built in 1789, to their current residence, a brick-red Georgian – the entirety of their careers – they have lived in and with the objects that propel their livelihood.

As I came to understand in my conversation with them, such immersion helps to build a broad comparative framework. True intimacy and expertise in a subject requires the passive absorption of subtleties only noticed by integrating those objects into daily life, not just in the office, but in the home. Put simply: The Snyders are good at what they do because they've made it a point to live with their collection.

And the chair. My photography subject for the next two days, and the reason I had come to see their collection in the first place, was sitting unceremoniously beside a window in the Snyders' front room. I was struck first by the chair's proportions. The chunky seat offset by lithe spindles. The arm that divides the comb at about a third of its height. The legs that are just a bit taller than the height of the seat to the top of the arm. A couple inches in any direction and the chair would have looked too narrow or too squat.

Then there was the crest rail. "Matisse!" I thought. It could have been cut from colored paper and pasted to a canvas like those blues and reds of *Panel with Mask*. So I named the chair Henry; the American cognation of the French artist's first name.

Henry is the Snyder's aesthetic in pine, maple, hickory, and crusty black paint. The couple seeks out antiques and art not simply because the pieces are rare or trendy or fit some staid archetype of what constitutes beauty. They seek out pieces that have character, and it is this character that makes the objects that the Snyders buy and sell so precious. Some may define character as a mash-up of whimsy, age, naivete, and imperfection. I see an object with character as something showcasing a personal, often experimental, sense of expression, one born from honesty, awareness, and expertise.

Before I set up my makeshift photo studio, I sat and talked with the Snyders at their dining room table. Why had this chair captivated them? Grace chimed in as she prepared a piece of 17th-century English needlework for display, "The imagination in country antiques, the connection with history and the maker – it's seeing individuals reinterpret standard forms. All of that opens up an interesting world. What's different about this chairmaker versus 99 percent of other chairmakers – what's definitive of this chairmaker – is that he saw the crest as a canvas to decorate." The crest rail, a piece of bent wood a bit over 2' long, speaks across the centuries through its wild, organic form.

In his slim but influential 1917 volume, *A Windsor Handbook*, Wallace Nutting mused on the value of Windsors, "Unfortunately mere rarity gives a large market value to antique furniture. But the collector ought to discriminate and not be led astray by rarity, even by uniqueness, unless the piece in question has other obvious merits....Quaintness, a quality hardly definable, but felt only, and by the lover of it only, is a quality much to be desired."[2]

Quaintness, I believe, is Nutting's version of character, with just a bit more mystique and erudite affect, but it highlights what experienced collectors know in their souls – that objects can speak to you, they can hit you square in the gut and in the heart. And the more people who are touched by the object, the more value it holds. Certain makers create objects with such resonance by chance, others with intention.

The Mystery of the Maker

Who was the 18th-century craftsman that fashioned this eccentric chair? Where did he live? Did he despise British rule? I found it impossible to resist the urge to speculate. As I photographed Henry, it became clear that there was one overwhelming truth: In an era of smoldering revolution, our craftsman was a creative rebel whose vision was realized at the intersection of expertise and experimentation.

As Henry was most likely made in the 1770s, it would have been impossible for our maker to avoid conversations about the Stamp Act of 1765, the Boston Massacre of 1770, the Intolerable Acts of 1774, or the Revolutionary War itself. Whether the chair was made on the eastern seaboard of Massachusetts or the outskirts of New Haven, such tumultuous times must have affected the way our maker framed his role in society, or at the very least, his notion of independence.

This is the very spirit Charles Santore addresses in his bible of Windsor chairmaking, *The Windsor Style in America*, writing that, "by the mid-1770s the American Windsor had reached its full development: the design was totally American, the stance was aggressive, the craftsmanship superb. It is not through ornamentation or decorative detail that we recognize the American Windsor but, rather, through the total spirit of its design. And I think that if that spirit could be summed up in a single word, that word would be *independence*."[3]

It's a romantic image, isn't it? A craftsman, buoyed by the conscious acts of rebellion that surround him, is given tacit permission to let his creative vision run free. He is liberated from traditional motifs and can experiment.

Perhaps there were clues within Henry's provenance that could anchor this conjecture. I asked the Snyders what they knew. Henry, to their knowledge, had been preserved by generations of the Pearson family in Essex County, Massachusetts, and the town of Byfield, in particular. Could our maker have lived in Massachusetts? Perhaps he was a Pearson himself.

Pearson is an ancient name in Massachusetts. It first surfaces in the 1640s in the villages of Reading and Rowley with two men, both named John. One, a deacon, settled in Rowley and built the first fulling mill in New England. The other, also involved in the church, was one of the seven heads of families that formed the First Church of Reading. (Rowley and Reading are 30 miles apart.) The former family has the Byfield connection, and so it is most likely that Henry belonged to generations of these Pearsons.

Thankfully, the historians of Essex County are diligent with their digitizing. I picked up a copy of *The Research Notes of Mary Adams Rolfe* from the Museum of Old Newbury's web archives, a document that has consolidated lineage and occupational records of the Pearson family from those first Johns, until the mid 19th century. Only one member of the Pearson family within our period of interest was associated with craft. Moses Pearson, born in 1697, is recorded as a joiner in the 1740s. He died in 1787 at 81 years old.

So, did Moses Pearson build Henry? He would have been 64 in 1770 – certainly an older man – but he was evidently in good health (he lived another 17 years). In the late 18th century, it was not uncommon for country joiners to be the woodworking generalists of their villages. While they may have lacked the outright turning or carving ability of formally trained turners or chairmakers, they would have had a shop equipped with a capable set of tools, and would have been familiar with the qualities of local timbers, basic turning, and the other techniques necessary to assemble a solid chair.

If Henry were built by a turner or chairmaker – even one from the country – we would expect the chair to have a set of baluster legs, arm posts, and standard bulbous stretchers (or at least a derivation of the typical form). The baluster turning motif was ubiquitous throughout the colonies, in urban centers and in rural villages, especially at the conclusion of the 18th century. There are hundreds of examples extant, with urban pieces normally being the most crisply turned, and rural examples the most playful. Henry's maker must have been aware of these trends.

But our chair's turnings are spare, ornamented only with a sharp double reel. This profile, on a Windsor, is exceedingly rare. So why did our maker not attempt to replicate the common baluster turnings, like so many of his fellow craftsmen did?

Joint Stool (1720–30) Pine top and frame; oak stretchers; one oak and three maple legs. 18-7/8" x 10-1/2" x 10-1/2" (47.9 x 26.7 x 26.7 cm). Mabel Brady Garvan Collection, Yale University Art Gallery. 1930.2135b.

Here I see three possible scenarios:

1. Henry was made by an adventurous chairmaker who liked to experiment with different turning profiles. He created the double-reel design, but found little commercial interest in it, only producing a few chairs with this form. Or those chairs he made with such a motif were for commission or personal use.

2. Henry was made by an adventurous and skilled joiner who dabbled in chairmaking. He created the double-reel motif because it added some ornament, but required less fuss than the complex undulations of the period's baluster profiles. It was a design born from necessary experimentation.

3. Henry's turnings are not unique to one maker, but we have simply lost other period examples due to fire, flood, termite attack, and paunchy uncles.

I see scenario two as most likely. The sheer rarity of Henry's turnings leads me to believe they were not the work of some prolific turner. The Snyders have seen one other chair with a similar design. And none in person. Searching through Nutting's books, Santore's books, a dozen or so other volumes on American Colonial furniture, auction records, and the vast expanse that is the internet, I found only two other pieces of seating with a similar double-reel motif. One was a riff on a joint stool (above, left), the other was a side chair – both are most likely Canadian.

The austerity of Henry's turnings leads me to believe that our maker was not a master of the lathe. Think of it this way: An 18th-century turner's sense of pride and fulfillment, whether he lived in the country or the city, would have come from his craft. His customers would have been exposed to, and enamored with, bold Philadelphia-style baluster turnings (evidenced by their popularity and export). Why wouldn't he want to showcase his skills and attempt to replicate the most celebrated expression of his craft? Why would he choose to create such spare turnings if he had the capability to do so much more?

As Peter Galbert, a contemporary master of the Windsor, notes in his *Chairmaker's Notebook*, "Of all the skills involved in chairmaking, turning sits apart. It is a separate skillset and will take time to master enough to keep pace with the other skills. It isn't unusual for someone to make fantastic spindles and carve a lovely seat but pair them with poor looking turnings."[4] And that is on a modern electric lathe.

Given the evidence, it seems likely that a country maker built Henry. That maker was evidently not a trained turner, and he, like Moses Pearson, most likely applied his skills to more than one trade, as was common in the time. It also seems likely that this maker built Henry in Connecticut, or at least lived in Connecticut for long enough to adopt its regional hallmarks.

Drawing by author.

    Back in western Massachusetts, on that hot summer afternoon in the Snyders' living room, Elliott brought out his copy of *The Windsor Style in America, Volume II*. There, on page 58, was a chair with nearly identical turnings and construction as Henry, attributed to a maker in Connecticut (above, left). There's no mention of eastern Massachusetts. The upturned ears of its crest rail and whimsy of its cutouts, plus the carved fan motif on its arms, the shape of the seat, and blind-socketed legs, are telltale signs of the Nutmeg State.
    Other details make the two seem more like fraternal twins than cousins. From the double-reel turnings on its legs and arm posts, to the seat shape and construction (grain orientation and those blind-socketed legs), and finally the crest rail, this chair is strikingly similar to Henry.
    The chances that two makers in different colonies would produce work that looked so similar, yet remain so uncommon, is astoundingly small. The rarity of Henry's decorative motifs throw coincidence out the window. There are dozens of Connecticut chairs from the early Windsor era that diverge remarkably from the standard Philadelphia forms – far more than those built in Massachusetts, especially outside of Boston where Henry lived for so many years. Patricia Kane, in *300 Years of American Seating Furniture*, is not alone in observing that there was "little doubt" in the "delight rural Connecticut taste found in fanciful ornament."[5]
    As for the suspected Pearson provenance, only if I were feeling particularly argumentative would I debate that the chair spent generations in eastern Massachusetts. As Dean Fales notes in *American Painted Furniture*, "In Windsors, however, one must always bear in mind that migration, emulation, and transportation can join together to provide as many exceptions as there are rules."[6] The Pearson family, like many 18th-century families, is notable for extensive "cousinage." There were a lot of them. And some, according to the family history, lived in Connecticut (Stonington, in particular). It is not difficult to imagine that Henry could have been purchased or bartered in Connecticut, then traveled up north with a Pearson to its long-term home by the sea. The wares of country makers did not always stay close to the site of their manufacture.
    What's most interesting about the disconnect between birthplace and eventual home is not that they are different locales, but rather that Henry wasn't scrapped, refinished, or otherwise disrespected through its life. The Pearsons had to make the effort to move it. They had to make the effort to keep it healthy through times of war, peace, feast, and famine. Can you imagine your great-grandchildren, and their children, respecting a piece of furniture you own as much as the Pearsons respected Henry? That respect wasn't merely a function of a perpetually disciplined household. Henry, by its very nature, demanded it.

The Windsor Stewards

Look at Henry again. Its survival is due to more than sheer necessity. Its poise, grounded yet airy, stately yet zany, surely made a statement in the home of its first owners – they must have loved it.

Perhaps its very existence is further proof of its Connecticut origins. Divergent and whimsical designs were hallmarks of the colony's craftsmen. Here, communities seemed to embrace the different, the fun, and the weird. And the tastes of those first owners were largely forged by the accepted norms of the communities in which they lived. It's human nature to deem something beautiful if society also deems it so. In close-knit 18th-century America, society was, by and large, the surrounding villages of hundreds, perhaps thousands.

As Santore notes, "These [early] unbranded chairs were conscientiously tailored to individual buyers, or they were produced by local craftsmen for a relatively small community. They incorporate regional style idiosyncrasies that, at their best, result in great American furniture design."[7]

Henry eventually found a loving home in Massachusetts and, evidently, its style did not offend the Commonwealth's sensibilities enough to end up a perversion of its former self. Blame it on Yankee practicality – no need to dispose of an object if it still serves a purpose. And the Windsor, in any derivation, is practical. "Many modern designers claim that a piece of furniture can be beautiful only if it is useful. The Windsor chair was one of the first designs of structure dictated by use."[8]

Henry is not the victim of what some collectors call benign neglect. It's worked for a living. That warm patina peeking through its black paint is not the product of some maniac with a sanding sponge. It's a luster made possible only by the grit of bodies – centuries of them. Henry isn't all flash and 18th-century Windsor psychedelia – it works. The Pearsons knew it, the Snyders knew it, and this unnaturally obsessed writer knew it the moment his glutes touched its old-growth white pine seat.

Elliott explained to me why they bought Henry. It existed as "one of the most imaginative versions of the thing." In this case, that imagination is made all the more exceptional when one considers the homogeneity of the Windsor form. So many of these chairs appear to be clones. Truly imaginative Windsors are rare. But that rarity, as mentioned earlier, is not the sole influencer of value. For Henry to merit its price tag, its character must match or exceed those two or three standard deviations from the norm. "Most of the time, experimentation is a failure," Elliott said, "but when it succeeds, it's brilliant." And Henry is brilliant. So much so that even an eye not trained in the ways of the Windsor can see it.

The impact is immediate and visceral. Our maker may have had a rebellious flair, but he appreciated balance and subtlety.

Henry, and other such examples of country furniture, are undervalued. Thanks to the shifting perceptions of history, craft, and form, it has become more than a chair – it revels in the fact it is not a sergeant in the clone army. Henry is convention, twisted and personalized. It is poetry, spoken to a packed house in some smoky Bowery bar. ◆

ENDNOTES

1. Grace and Elliott Snyder, collectors and dealers, interview by Nathaniel Brewster in South Egremont, Massachusetts, July 26-27. 2018.
2. Wallace Nutting, *A Windsor Handbook* (Saugus, MA: Wallace Nutting, Inc., 1917), 91.
3. Charles Santore, *The Windsor Style in America: The Definitive Pictorial Study of the History and Regional Characteristics of the Most Popular Furniture Form of 18th Century America 1730-1840* (Vol 1 & 2) (Philadelphia: Courage Books, 1997), 45.
4. Peter Galbert, *Chairmaker's Notebook* (Fort Mitchell, KY: Lost Art Press, 2015), 183.
5. Patricia E. Kane, *300 Years of American Seating Furniture, Chairs and Beds from the Mabel Brady Garvan and Other Collections at Yale University* (New York: New York Graphic Society, 1976), 66.
6. Dean Fales Jr., *American Painted Furniture 1660-1880* (New York: Dutton, 1972), 87.
7. Santore, *The Windsor Style in America*, 44.
8. Ralph and Terry Kovel, *American Country Furniture 1780-1875* (New York: Crown, 1972), 113.

William Morris Gallery, London Borough of Waltham Forest.

WILLIAM MORRIS & GEORGE NAKASHIMA

Finding the Middle Landscape

David Lane

Courtesy of George Nakashima Woodworkers.

"If a designer is completely honest with his materials, he ends up with a solution similar to someone else's, even though he is separated by 100 miles or 100 years."

– George Nakashima[1]

Photos: Michael J. Joniec. Courtesy of Moderne Gallery.

At the Minnesota Landscape Arboretum's Andersen Horticultural Library, you will find a suite of library tables and reading chairs designed by George Nakashima, one of the leading woodworkers and furniture designers of the 20th century. His most renowned and influential contribution was to make use of a board's natural edge by carefully removing the bark to reveal the gorgeous undulations below the cambium layer. Additionally, he respected the wood's natural flaws and did not shy away from incorporating knots or checks into a beautifully finished piece.

Nakashima was influenced by Sōetsu Yanagi, considered the father of the *mingei* (folk craft) revival in Japan and founder of the Japanese Folk Crafts Museum in 1936. Yanagi was in turn significantly influenced by both John Ruskin and William Morris. British potter Bernard Leach, Yanagi's lifelong friend who translated his most famous work, *The Unknown Craftsman*, recollected that "naturally the English movement under William Morris was the subject of much discussion."[2] Writing for the *Journal of the William Morris Society*, Yuko Kikuchi concludes that "Yanagi, Ruskin and Morris certainly shared the same ideas. They all prized craftsmanship and handcrafts. They were all medievalists, having as their ideal a society in which art and morality were united."[3] Nakashima was deeply influenced by Yanagi's philosophy and even followed his example of the unknown craftsman by not signing his work until, ironically with his own pieces gaining recognition for their innovation and beauty, clients demanded that he sign his work so that they could prove their provenance. And although Yanagi studied, gathered, and promoted the handcrafts of his countrymen, he was not himself a craftsman. Morris and Nakashima's shared lifelong commitment to producing objects of beauty in an increasingly industrialized and mass-produced world laid the foundation for the parallels in their working lives. The four most significant similarities are that each man valued the past (specifically the medieval guilds), practiced then moved away from architecture, pursued a pastoral ideal based on a deep love of nature, and reconciled technology and handcrafted production.

Valuing the Past

Both men valued the pre-industrial past, as evidenced by what truly is a coincidence: They both visited Belgium's Bruges Cathedral. Morris had been there for the first of several visits in 1854 and, as described by his lifelong colleague Phillip Webb, "this place was one of the towns which always gave William Morris pleasure."[4] Nakashima, upon his visit in the late 1920s, was equally delighted. He described it as "thirteenth century France in all its glory. The peak of Western culture."[5] Contrasted with the increased specialization and separation of design from making that characterized both men's times, Bruges represented an era of guild workmanship and communal accomplishment in seeing a project through from beginning to end. Nakashima believed that "in ages past, it would have been easy to join a crusade, to become a member of a community dedicated to building a great cathedral, to hew the great timbered doors, to carve a spirit in stone to grace the glorious facade."[6] Morris and his compatriots demonstrated this admiration not only by joining the Medieval Society in 1858 but also by designing Morris' first residence and artists' commune, Red House, with numerous medieval architectural and design motifs. Many of the tapestries and stained-glass pieces from this time reflect Morris' passion for those "days bygone."[7]

Importantly, it is also true that Bruges Cathedral and all it represented did not trap either man in the past. As will be discussed in detail, neither shied away from new technologies that promised to improve the efficiency of their operations, and both men succeeded in innovation and originality. Morris, in his lecture "The Lesser Arts," recommended that his contemporaries "study ancient arts wisely, be taught by it, kindled by it; all the while determining not to imitate or repeat it; to have either no art at all, or an art which we have made our own."[8] Nakashima's reputation for innovation was widely recognized "as offering a viable alternative and model to furniture makers working within an industry dominated by mass-produced furniture."[9] His live-edged tables, desks, and cabinets presented something completely new while retaining the same spirit in wood as in the stone that graced the medieval cathedrals he so admired.

Architecture to Craftsmanship

Their initial forays into architectural careers reflect similar motivations and influences in their decisions to become designer-craftsmen instead. For Morris, his employment with the architectural firm of George Street was brief, lasting just one year, proving too restrictive to Morris' restless nature. Philip Webb, a colleague at the firm who later became a partner at Morris' own firm, Morris, Marshall, Faulkner & Co., spoke of "how unsuited Morris was to the disciplines and tediums of office life."[10] It is also likely that Morris recognized early on the value he placed on being more directly connected to the results of his labor, "challenging accepted social patterns by involving himself in the process of handwork."[11] Drawing window elevations all day without seeing the overall context or final product was unacceptable and so, in late 1856,

Morris left Street's firm.

A similar trend was occurring in postwar America in the mid-20th century where the advent of mass production, specialization, and new materials alienated artist/designers from the production process. As American industrial designer Don Wallance stated in his 1956 study *Shaping America's Products*, "Once design became self-conscious, through being made the specialized task of the 'artist,' who did not himself actually work at the wheel or bench or lathe, the spontaneous taste of the craftsman was inevitably undermined."[12] Nakashima responded to this alienation by seeking out a more scalable and creative life, finding that he "preferred the materiality of furniture making to the frequent separation of architectural design from the act of building."[13]

Both men were outspoken in their disenchantment with contemporary architecture. Nakashima saw the building craze of his time as a threat to society's very soul and spiritual survival:

Backed into a soulless steel and glass jungle...we face an unknown future. With a prodigious drive we have built the first megalopolis, but we have produced so little of any intrinsic value. Taken as a whole, we have the poorest assemblage of architecture in the history of man, without a single building of greatness.[14]

Morris was no less strident in his condemnation of the building craze in the London of his day:

Yet little does that help us in these days when, if a man leaves England for a few years, he finds when he comes back half a county of bricks and mortar added to London. Can the greatest optimists say that the style of building in that half county has improved meanwhile? Is it not true, on the contrary, that it goes on getting worse, if that be possible? the last house built being always the vulgarest and ugliest...[15]

The rush of 19th-century industrialization and, a century later, rapid urban growth and the trend toward "steel and glass" drove both men away from architecture to a more controllable scale of craftsmanship.

The Middle Landscape

The parallels between Morris and Nakashima can also be framed around a seminal study of the relationship between England and America's ideal of "pastoralism" and the intrusion of industrialization and commercialism on that ideal. Leo Marx's *The Machine in the Garden* analyzes the rise of industrialism in England and America as documented through the literature of the 19th and early 20th centuries. For Marx, pastoralism is an attitude toward the land and a way of life in which rural ideals of nature, self-sufficiency, and simplicity rule; one that was strongly encouraged by the seemingly vast and fantastically rich landscape of the American colonies and the growing nation. The threat to this ideal took the form of rapid technological and industrial growth, one in which "within the lifetime of a single generation, a rustic and in large part wild landscape was transformed into the site of the world's most productive industrial machine."[16] In England as well, this transformation was rapid and disruptive. As early as the 1820s the social critic Thomas Carlyle lamented that "our old modes of exertion are all discredited, and thrown aside. On every hand, the living artisan is driven from his workshop, to make room for a speedier, inanimate one."[17]

By the middle of the 19th century, Morris saw steam power both on the railroad and within factories rapidly become the dominant threat to his pre-industrial goals for creativity and production. A century later, as Nakashima came into his own as a designer and craftsman, the post-World War II surge in technologies derived from the war effort, from plastics to plywood, combined with the rise in commercialism, created a similar threat to his method of handwork and design. Commenting on the disconnect between the designer and consumer, Dan Wallance observed that as the "salesman became the focal point of mass distribution, the direct contact between the designer-maker and the user of his products was destroyed."[18] That close relationship was critical to Nakashima who designed and selected the wood for his best pieces based on consultations with his clients.

Both men responded with a mixture of rebelliousness and strategic acceptance of the reality of their day. They sought what Marx documents as "the middle landscape," a balance in which technology and market forces are counterbalanced by the humanizing effects of nature and handwork.[19] To a degree, both men succeeded, though not without compromise.

Their pursuit of this middle landscape had deep roots in the beneficence of nature. Morris' early years in the 1840s at his home in Walthamstow were a time of discovery and joy as he explored and studied the wildlife, trees, and plants in and around Epping Forest.[20] Many of the decorative designs for which he became so well-known harked back to images retained in his mind's eye from his fascination with the flora and fauna of his childhood. The forest held recuperative value for Nakashima as well. In *The Soul of a Tree*, he described his youth among the trees and mountains of his native Washington State with longing:

During the long hikes down, I never failed to be struck by na-

William Morris' Workshop at Merton Abbey (Watercolor by Lexden Louis Pocock, 1880) © Victoria and Albert Museum, London.

Main Shop. George Nakashima Woodworkers. New Hope, Pennsylvania.

ture's many moods – the harsh reality of the stunted trees at the timberline hanging by threads of roots to small crevices; then the moss hanging from deep in the tops of trees in the rain forest of the Ho Valley, where only the slenderest shafts of light reached the ground; finally the great cathedral of magnificent trees, straight and taut, fully ten feet in diameter. These were my personal relationships – ones I would cherish through the years."[21]

As these two artist-craftsmen matured, they sought out the natural world as an escape from the intrusion of urbanism with what they perceived as its soul-crushing and dehumanizing force. Nakashima settled with his family in the rural town of New Hope, Pennsylvania, and eventually built his home and workshop there. He referred to New Hope as "our redoubt, our last stand against mediocrity in our system. It was nice to go it alone, to forge a life in the wilderness, to fight against commercialism and bigness."[22] His attachment to nature was further reinforced by visits to his ancestral home of Japan, where Zen Buddhism traditions affirmed man's interdependence and oneness with nature. The visit reinforced a spiritual awakening centered on the fact that not only humans but all of nature – including trees – have a soul. He lived by that creed all his life.

Morris' circumstance was more complex due to his business interests requiring a proximity to a commercial center such as London. Nonetheless, he sought out locations that offered access to wilderness and a refuge from "the alienating city to the human scale of the landscape in the country."[23] Red House, the first home he built as both family home and artists' commune, was in the rural hamlet of Blexleyheath, ten miles from London. Later, in 1881, he tolerated a two-hour commute from his Hammersmith home to the Morris & Co. factory at Merton, specifically chosen for its pastoral setting along the Wandle River. His business manager, George Wardle, observed, "It is noticeable perhaps, in remembering his nervous temperament, that though he disliked the journey from Hammersmith intensely…he showed no sign of irritation on arriving. The latter part of the journey, perhaps, through the fields, was soothing and then there was the short passage from the station through the garden of the Abbey and the prospect of being soon at work which together may have restored his equilibrium."[24]

Nakashima and Morris both sought and found peace in nature. Building on this core value they then attempted to find that "middle landscape" for creating and marketing handcrafted products in an industrialized, commercial society.

The Machine in the Garden

The first challenge both men experienced was the exponential development of machine technology which began in earnest during Morris' generation and continued on through Nakashima's. Nakashima, Morris, and Ruskin before them, recognized that handwork, especially when undertaken with creativity and individuality, infused the work with both a tangible sense of human input and with a level of detail and quality that distinguished it from mass-produced machine work. That unique human quality went missing from machine-produced furniture because the latter relied on standardized dimensioning; repeatability; and mass-produced, surface-mounted ornamentation. Morris saw no future in these processes. In his 1884 lecture, "Useful Work versus Useless Toil," he optimistically predicted the demise of machinery, which "would probably, after a time, be somewhat restricted when men found out that there was no need for anxiety as to mere subsistence and learned to take an interest and pleasure in handiwork which, done deliberately and thoughtfully, could be made more attractive than machine work."[25]

Nakashima straight-back chair. Photo: Michael J. Joniec.
Courtesy of Moderne Gallery.

Morris Sussex Armchair. Catalogue Number G55.
Willliam Morris Gallery, London Borough of Waltham Forest.

Nakashima similarly believed that quality and beauty were not programmed by a technician but rather the result of decades of tradition and skill. In his description of true craftsmanship, "the woodworker is completely dedicated, with a strong sense of vocation. Often his craft has been handed down from generation to generation. A woodworker's hands develop in a special way with intense and concentrated use. The flesh becomes stronger and heavier in certain areas, better fitted to grasp and use the tools. He has a special intensity, a striving for perfection, a conviction that any task must be executed with all his skill."[26] Such "intensity" could not be automated, just as the "interest and pleasure" Morris referred to could have no meaning for a machine.

However, neither man was blind to the potential for machines to increase efficiency by handling the less creative and more repetitive tasks of production. To compete successfully in the commercial and industrialized marketplace, they both recognized the need for a middle ground in which machines might help narrow the gap in costs between shoddy and quality production. Morris installed the more automated Jacquard looms at Merton Abbey, thus increasing the pattern range and efficiency of brocades and other woven goods. Nakashima had close relationships with large automated milling operations and made use of power equipment in his workshop for sanding and shaping components.

The key was to achieve a "synthesis between the hand and the machine."[27] As long as the worker maintained control over the machine rather than becoming a tool of the machine itself, he could continue to impart his human skill and judgment while effectively utilizing machines. In a 1953 interview with the *New York Herald Tribune*, Nakashima suggested that "we must adapt to our experiences and our technology. To accomplish this, as I see it, a whole new environment has to be created, an environment not based on the sentiments of the spinning wheel but also not based on sentiments and tyrannies of the production line. Rather an environment which provides a synthesis of what is good for us as human beings, who are in control of their environment, not victims of it."[28] This is the difficult "middle landscape" Marx identified and which, a century earlier, Morris bemoaned as slipping away with rising industrialization. Overall, both Morris and Nakashima succeeded in finding their middle landscape.

Competing in the marketplace nonetheless had its realities. The high cost of these handcrafted, even if machine-assisted, products made them available only to a wealthy elite able to afford the cost of hand-printed wall papers or hand-jointed tables of elm, laurel, and English burl oak. It is unlikely an average consumer could have afforded a single item from Nakashima's 1974 commission to build a suite of furniture for Nelson Rockefeller's Pocantico Hills compound. For Morris, for whom bringing art and quality handicrafts to the general population was a social cause, the exclusivity of Morris & Co. products was a disturbing compromise.

They addressed these issues in part by collaborating with the very institutions they deplored, whose production volume and technology could hold down costs. In the 1870s, Morris succeeded in producing an affordable and well-designed product with the Sussex line of chairs and settees. While designed by Morris & Co., the chairs were built by outside manufacturers whose factories had access to steam-bending and turning machinery. The chairs were some of the most popular of all Morris & Co. products and were listed in the company catalog beyond Morris' death into the early 1900s.

Nakashima broadened the market for his designs by entering into a business agreement in 1946 with the large furniture manufacturer Knoll. His designs included several lines of chairs and small tables mass-produced and marketed by Knoll but for which he retained the rights to produce by hand in his own workshop.[29] The furniture line greatly augmented Nakashima's visibility in the market and, while the pieces were not inexpensive, they were more affordable than the custom pieces from his workshop. By 1954, however, this collaboration had run its course and Nakashima returned to uniquely designed pieces built in his New Hope studio. As with Morris, Nakashima walked the line between "artistic integrity and commercial necessity...fighting as much against the market as working with it."[30]

A Community of Craftsmen

Lastly, both men saw the value of creating a community of craftsmen rather than an assembly line of specialized laborers. For Morris, this was a social cause founded in Ruskin's belief that joy in labor was critical to preserving art within society. For Nakashima, the integration of art and labor followed from the spiritual depth he encouraged in his workshop. In their own ways, both men succeeded within the limits of economic necessity.

By today's standards Morris' commitment seems almost to good to be true. In his essay "The Factory as it Might Be," Morris stated, "A factory might not only be pleasant as to its surroundings and beautiful in its architecture, but that even the rough and necessary work done in it might be so arranged as to be neither burdensome in itself nor of long duration for each worker. But furthermore, the organization of such a factory – that is to say, a group of people working in harmonious co-operation toward a useful end – would of itself afford opportunities for increasing the pleasure of life."[31] Merton Abbey was the closest he came to achieving this ideal, with its idyllic setting in which the "low long buildings with the clear rushing little stream running between them, and

William Morris Workers at Merton (Block Printing Workshop). Courtesy of Merton Working Heritage, London.

Richard Ganor, Craftsman. Courtesy of George Nakashima Woodworkers.

David Mellor Round Building. Courtesy of David Mellor Design Museum, Hathersage, Hope Valley, England.

the wooden outside staircases leading to their upper storey, have nothing about them to suggest the modern factory."[32] More than the physical building, however, Morris was committed to understanding every process in which his workers engaged, an extraordinary accomplishment considering this meant mastering such skills as weaving, dyeing, stained glass and tile work, block printing, and embroidery. While it is true that commercial requirements led to compromises in which his workers had little opportunity to express themselves creatively, his leadership and involvement with their work won him high praise: "Dressed in a workman's blouse, his hands stained with dyes, Morris shared the labor and understood the culture of his men...although he paid by the piece and bypassed apprenticeship rules, his enthusiasm made up for any deficiencies in labor conditions."[33]

Nakashima's workshop of 10 to 20 workers was considerably smaller than Morris & Co. and it may have been easier to promote in his employees a sense of ownership and contribution. Being strongly spiritually oriented, he set a standard based on an ego-transcending Eastern philosophy in which "each woodworker is an individual craftsman, free to work out his own *sadhana*, spiritual training to attain deep concentration resulting in union with the ultimate reality. Each person can do what he finds most suitable within certain guidelines."[34] His ideal of a community of workers was not without compromise, however, as he maintained strict control over design and production decisions. He had little if any tolerance for anything short of the highest-quality craftsmanship. According to his daughter, Mira Nakashima, who took over after his death, "Two aspects of Nakashima's character must be acknowledged before either the man or his work can be properly understood. One of these was the *yin* aura of peace and serenity that seemed to permeate his work....The other was the *yang* of highly disciplined authoritarianism, a simmering violence that erupted most often in dealing with family and shop members."[35] Fortunately, as evidenced by the decades-long tenure of many of his workers (foreman Gerald Everett, still with the firm, was hired in 1970), yin and yang were kept in balance by the rewards of participating in the creation of beautifully crafted work.

The Model Today

The overriding theme connecting Morris and Nakashima, one that can be found even today during the "Third Industrial Revolution" of 3D printers and CNC lasers, is their commitment to beauty and spirit, and each man's assurance that those qualities can be infused into everyday objects by the application of the human hand, by craftsmanship. Two examples support this conclusion.

The David Mellor Cutlery Factory in Hathersage, England, produces award-winning cutlery and silver that is sold in the finest shops worldwide. Corin Mellor, son of the founder, is involved in both design and production, and many of the employees have been with the factory for decades. The factory itself is an award-winning structure, well-stocked with machinery arranged in a sequence that flows in a circle from stamping blanks to polishing. Set within the Peak District National Park, the Round Building is the very definition of pastoralism, a functioning example of the "machine in the garden."

Thos. Moser, Auburn, Maine, holds a reputation for producing some of the finest residential and commercial furniture available. A family business in the same tradition of Morris, Nakashima, and the Mellors, the Mosers involve their workers to the point of having the persons responsible for a particular piece sign that piece upon completion. Their standards are based on "a legacy of beautiful forms executed by hand and built to last for generations...conceived to offer service and beauty."[36] In words that could have been spoken by Morris, Thomas Moser sums up the philosophy of all the craftsmen mentioned in this article: "It is craftsmanship that birthed our company, and it is craftsmanship that continues to nourish it."[37] ◆

Thomas Moser signing a chair. Courtesy of Thos. Moser Furniture, Auburn, Maine.

ENDNOTES

1. Mira Nakashima, *Nature, Form & Spirit: The Legacy of George Nakashima*. (New York: Harry N. Abrams, 2003), 122.
2. Sōetsu Yanagi, *The Unknown Craftsman: A Japanese Insight into Beauty* (Tokyo: Kodansha International, 1972), 94.
3. Yuko Kikuchi, "A Japanese William Morris: Yanagi Sōetsu and Mingei Theory," *The Journal of the William Morris Society*, 12/2, Spring 1997, 39-45.
4. Fiona MacCarthy, *William Morris: A Life for Our Time* (New York: Knopf, 1995), 152.
5. George Nakashima, *The Soul of a Tree* (Tokyo, New York: Kodansha International, 1981), 51.
6. Ibid., 109.
7. William Morris, "Under an Elm-Tree; or, Thoughts in the Country-Side," *Commonweal* 5, No. 182, 6 July, 1889, 212. http://www.marxists.org/archive/morris/works/1889/commonweal/ 07-elm-tree.htm.
8. William Morris, "The Lesser Arts," Lecture delivered December 4, 1877, *Hopes and Fears for Art* (London: Longmans, Green and Co., 1908), 20. https://archive.org/details/ hopesfearsforart00morrrich.
9. Gay MacDonald, "The 'Advance' of American Postwar Design in Europe: MoMA and the Design for Use, 1951-1953," *Design Issues*, 24/2, Spring 2008, 23. http://www.jstor.org/stable/25224164.
10. MacCarthy, *William Morris: A Life for Our Time*, 104.
11. Ibid., 175.
12. Don Wallance, *Shaping America's Products* (New York: Reinhold, 1956), 12.
13. Steven Beyer, *George Nakashima and the Modernist Moment* (Doylestown, PA: James A. Michener Art Museum, 2001), 22.
14. Nakashima, *The Soul of a Tree*, 193.
15. William Morris, "Art, Wealth and Riches," Lecture delivered March 6, 1883, *Architecture, Industry & Wealth: Collected Papers* (London: Longmans, Green and Co., 1902), 86. https://archive.org/details/.
16. Leo Marx, *The Machine in the Garden* (Oxford: Oxford University Press, 1964), 343.
17. Thomas Carlyle, "Signs of the Times," *Edinburgh Review*, 1829, *Critical and Miscellaneous Essays by Thomas Carlyle*, Vol. 5 (Boston: Phillips, Sampson & Co., 1855), 188.
18. Wallance, *Shaping America's Products*, 12.
19. Marx, *The Machine in the Garden*, 160.
20. Blue Calhoun, *The Pastoral Vision of William Morris: The Earthly Paradise* (Athens: University of Georgia Press, 1975), 10.
21. Nakashima, *The Soul of a Tree*, 47.
22. Kate Holland Gormley, "The Soul of a Craftsman," *The Bloedel Reserve Newsletter*, 13/1, Spring 2001, 6.
23. MacCarthy, *William Morris: A Life for Our Time*, 604.
24. David Saxby, *William Morris at Merton* (London: Museum of London Archaeology Service, 1995), 14.
25. William Morris, "Useful Work versus Useless Toil," Lecture delivered in 1884, *Signs of Change: Seven Lectures* (London: Longmans, Green and Co., 1903), 170. https://archive.org/details/signsofchangesev00morr.
26. Nakashima, *The Soul of a Tree*, 113.
27. David Kimmerly and Catherine C. Lavoie, *George Nakashima Woodworker Complex, National Register of Historic Places Registration Form* (Washington: National Park Service, 2013), 28.
28. Ibid., 29.
29. Mira Nakashima, *Nature, Form & Spirit*, 76.
30. Charles Harvey and Jon Press, "John Ruskin and the Ethical Foundations of Morris & Company, 1861-96," *Journal of Business Ethics*, 14/3, March 1995, 187. http://www.jstor.org/stable/25072636.
31. William Morris, "The Factory as It Might Be," first published in *Justice*, April-May 1884, in *Factory Work as It Is and Might Be: A Series of Four Papers by William Morris* (New York: New York Labor News Co., 1922), 25. https://archive.org/details/factoryworkasit00morrgoog.
32. Saxby, *William Morris at Merton*, 15.
33. Eileen Boris, *Art & Labor: Ruskin, Morris and the Craftsman Ideal in America* (Philadelphia: Temple University Press, 1986), 9.
34. Nakashima, *The Soul of a Tree*, 138.
35. Mira Nakashima, *Nature, Form & Spirit*, 116.
36. Thomas Moser, "Mission Statement," Thomas Moser Furniture Cabinetmakers, 2014. http://www.thosmoser.com/page.php?page_id=54. [Last accessed November 21, 2014].
37. Thomas Moser, "A Word from Tom," *Product Catalog*, Spring 2015, 3.

Opposite: Willliam Morris Gallery, London Borough of Waltham Forest.

Examination *of an* 1804 Painted Cupboard

Purchased at an antiques fair, this early 19th-century cupboard is said to have originated in Pennsylvania. The bold paint scheme, pegged (wooden nail) construction, and irregular primary and secondary surfaces create a unique piece for study.

Private collection.

Top shows scalloped plane tracks.

One-board back fastened with wooden nails. Hanging hardware later attached with wire nails.

Bottom. Original side repair shown at right.

WOOD: Unidentified softwood

DIMENSIONS:

Height overall: 22-1/4"
Width overall: (top) 21-5/8", (case) 15-1/4"
Depth overall: (top) 11-3/4", (case) 8-7/8"
Door: 15-3/8" wide x 13-1/4" high x 1/2" thick

Side thickness: 3/4"
Shelf thickness: 11/16"
Back thickness: 1/2" ± (varies)

Plane tracks on case side.
Wooden nails seen.

Lid shown from underside. Sawn out of square before thumbnail molding shaped.

Original strap hinges. Dovetailed batten repair seen between hinges.

Paint decoration on door.

Handmade escutcheon.

Clinched nails exit through door face.

Grain-painted side.

Abandoned saw cuts for hinges on opposite side match existing hinges exactly.

Cornice molding shown from rear.

Wooden nails fasten molding.

Wooden nails on backboard.

Wooden nails broken through bottom board inside case.

Small shelf with notches made from leftover molding from front.

Wooden nails holding cornice molding protrude inside case.

Scars from toothed bench hook on end grain of side board.

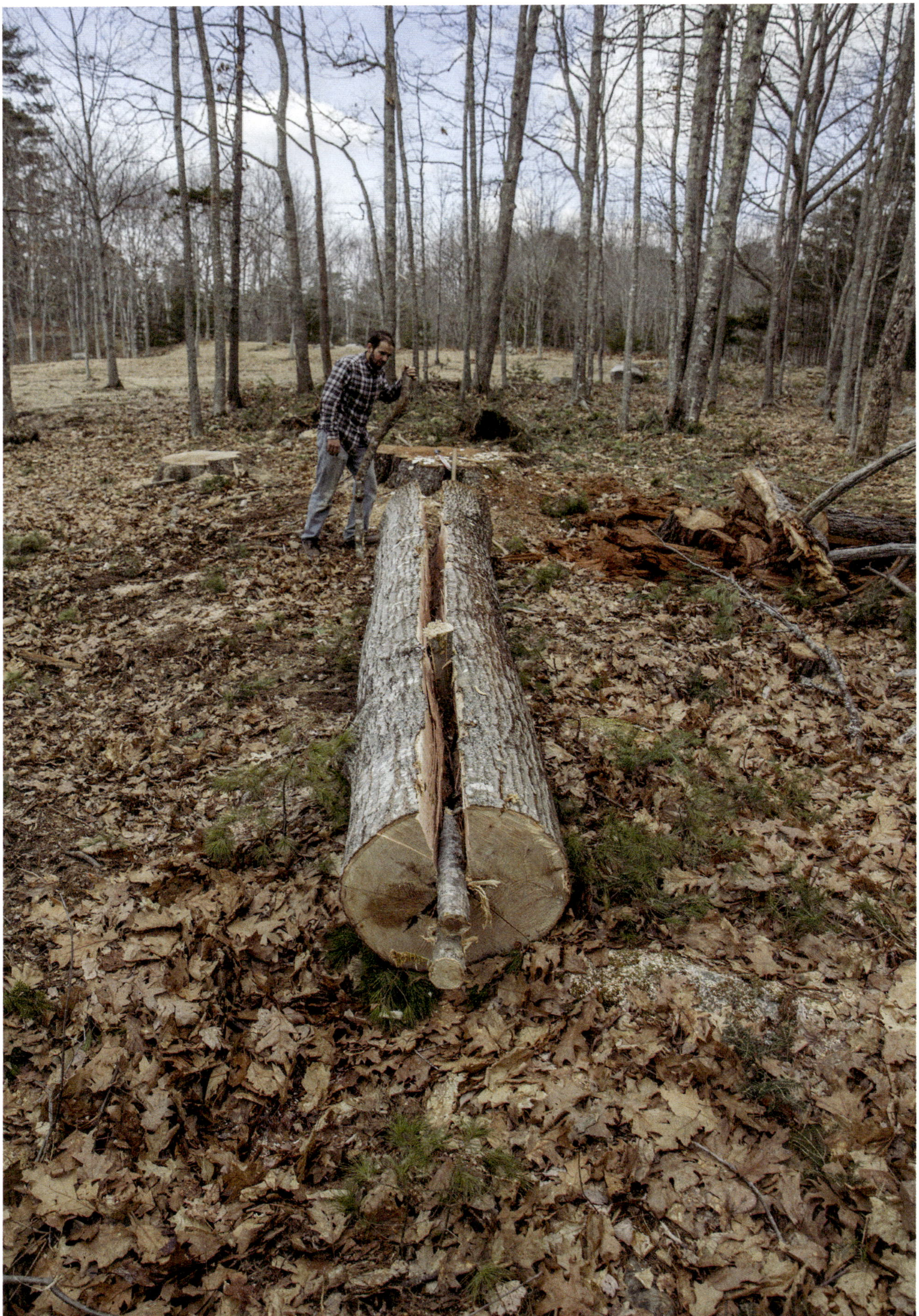

A TALE *of* TWO TREES
The Radical Efficiency of Green Woodworking

Michael Updegraff

"Good workmanship – that is, careful, considerate, and loving work – requires us to think considerately of the whole process, natural and cultural, involved in the making of wooden artifacts, because the good worker does not share the industrial contempt for 'raw material.' The good worker loves the board before it becomes a table, loves the tree before it yields the board, loves the forest before it gives up the tree."

– Wendell Berry

The importance of the relationship that humans share with trees cannot be overstated. Simply put, we owe our survival as a species almost entirely to these plants, and from our most ancient past we have held trees in the highest esteem. Consider the Tree of the Knowledge of Good and Evil in the Garden of Eden, or the great ash *Yggdrasil* in Norse mythology that holds the nine realms together, or the sacred fig (*Ficus religiosa*) that Buddha sat under. Trees provide us with our primary shelter-building material, giving poles for tipis, timbers for barns, and even peeled veneers for plywood. Every culture has produced household goods primarily out of wood and, until the Industrial Revolution, it was our primary fuel source for heating and cooking. But unlike any of our other raw materials, trees are capable of renewing and regenerating themselves endlessly. "Imagine a steelworks run entirely on solar energy, producing all its own solar panels and making no noise," writes green woodworker Mike Abbott, "or a plastics factory that actually purified the atmosphere and required at most only a few hours' human input a year; picture a fibre-glass works supporting all kinds of wildlife where people would drive for miles to spend a day strolling around the production unit."[1]

As I write, I am looking out into the woods that surround our house. The year's leaves have fallen, opening a window to the stream as it winds its way back toward the beaver pond and allowing me to pick out the evergreen balsam firs growing on the hill. The deciduous trees here (maple, ash, birch, oak) are at rest after quietly working all summer, drawing water up from their roots and carbon dioxide out of the air through their leaves to photosynthesize the sugars that are used to build new wood cells. These cells form a new growth ring around the circumference of the tree beneath the bark – a few fractions of an inch per year – as well as expanding the tree's crown and root system.

Oxygen is the primary waste product of this marvelous process, along with the spent leaves which, after a fiery autumn show, settle back to the forest floor to build loam and replenish nutrients. "Because the process of wood production continues quietly, cleanly and with very little need for human intervention, we take it very much for granted. But if we lived in a world relying totally on steel, plastic, and fibre-glass, where wood was unknown, imagine the public acclaim if some scientist were suddenly to invent a tree!"[2] Every virtue of the various species that we as woodworkers love – strength, hardness, workability, striking figure – is derived from the forest environment, from the way they generate new cellulose, deal with stress, and compete in the climb skyward after the sun. It follows, then, that if we want to grow in our knowledge and understanding of working wood, we should learn to see the forest for the trees.

Forest to Table

For all that modern technology and infrastructure offer us, they excel (for better or worse) at separating us from the sources of our basic necessities. We live in a day and age where our food comes from the supermarket, gasoline from the pump, and light in our homes from the flip of a switch (or a polite command to a smart speaker). The average Westerner lives a life far more comfortable than any king of past ages enjoyed. It's quite easy to take this intricate supply chain for granted, to be completely dependent upon it, a fact we all come to grips with when we suffer a prolonged power outage or a weather event that depletes local grocery store shelves. Suddenly, we feel the weight of this dependency.

As woodworkers, we might think we're getting a leg-up on this condition by building our own furniture. "I don't need any of that big-box, flat-pack, pressboard-and-laminate rubbish that everyone else calls a 'bookshelf,'" we think to ourselves, "I'll build my own!" And so we do – carefully picking through a selection of kiln-dried, machined boards at the home-improvement warehouse, setting aside anything with the slightest twist or cantankerous grain. But, in reality, this makes us only a little more extricated from the supply chain, hardly closer to that tree in the forest, than our friends with their newly assembled Swedish furniture.

Not many generations ago, our ancestors lived much closer to the natural world, to the woods and soil, and knew how to efficiently process raw materials into the necessities of life. These skills allowed a craftsman to "build their own house, make all the house tools and instruments, the cart, the sledge and the footwear; his wife will knit the necessary clothes for her husband and children and all the linen needed in the house."[3] This level of knowledge was not extraordinary for the day, but relatively basic for the rural farmer. As Roy Underhill has noted, "Clearing land, splitting fence rails, shaving shovel handles, bending oxbows – there are few aspects of woodworking unfamiliar to the countryman. He fells the hickory, splits it and shaves it to make a chair, strips its bark to weave the chair bottom, and sits in it by a fire fueled by the limbs."[4] The supply chain contained just one link – the maker. Outside city centers and before industrialization, the specialist would have had little practical value.

The back-to-the-land movement (as well as more recent offshoots such as the farm-to-table trend in dining) seeks to short-circuit the elaborate industrial complex that produces most of our consumable and durable goods these days. Proponents of the philosophy point to the loss of skill that is evident in the average person for basic tasks; to the health and environmental effects of large-scale industrialization; and to the sociological harm that comes of being dependent on technologies that are beyond the control or comprehension of most individuals.[5] This dependence becomes crippling when a technological or supply-chain disruption renders us incapable of executing those basic tasks that we have turned over to mechanization. Even as we enjoy the benefits and ease that these technologies offer on a day-to-day basis, it would be wise to contemplate what we might be losing in this transaction as a culture, as individuals, and as woodworkers.

This is a tale of two trees – or rather, a tale of two ways we might go about processing them into the materials we need to create things. One way is wholly modern, relying on the many advances in science and technology that we currently enjoy, to process the "stuff" of a tree into the dry, stable, predictably cuboid stock of our local home center or lumberyard. The second approach is far older, and necessitates a more intimate, visceral, and, frankly, sweaty process to work out the stock we need. Wood is a wild material not easily tamed, but seeking to understand the substance of it at a deeper level, beginning with the tree in the forest, can be an immensely rewarding task with distinct practical advantages.

The term "green woodworking" was coined in the late 1970s as the back-to-the-land movement began to knock on the door of what had become mainstream woodworking practice – using power tools to shape machine-dimensioned stock. Pioneers such as Roy Underhill, Drew and Louise Langsner, and others began exploring and writing about the old ways of creating wooden objects, beginning at the stump. Langsner first settled on the phrase "country woodcraft" to describe this idea in his 1978 book of the same name. But as he tells it, "One early reader of the book was John Alexander, a Baltimore chair maker....John pointed out that the term 'country woodcraft' excludes someone like him, working in the basement of an inner-city row house, whereas in fact many crafts that are now considered 'country' were also the work of village and urban craftspeople....John suggested a substitute term, 'green woodworking.'"[6] The name stuck.

The "green" in green woodworking wasn't meant as a descriptor of environmental or ecological friendliness (although this is a striking aspect of it, as we will see), but is simply the state of the wood when it first gets in the hands of the maker. Alexander uses the term "wet woodworking" in the classic *Make a Chair From a Tree* – a suitable (if less catchy) way to describe a process quite distinct from using kiln-dried, dimensioned stock. "Green or wet means wood that still contains most of the water it had while alive. Wet woodworking requires an understanding of the unique way wood shrinks as it dries."[7] Green wood can contain two-thirds water by weight, and is far more easily worked with hand tools than is dried lumber. But you can't turn your back on it. As it dries, a board can warp, check, and writhe around on the bench like the living thing that it is, driving the uninitiated to tears. A deeper understanding of the material is necessary for success. This knowledge of the properties of raw wood, grasped and utilized by humankind for millenia, has waned dramatically since the Industrial Revolution.

Lumber Today

Even the most highly processed composite wood product today still begins with the tree. Often grown on managed land, trees to be used for lumber are carefully selected by forestry technicians. If no road exists in the area, one is bulldozed into the forest. The trees are felled, bucked to length, and transported via diesel skidders to a staging area, where they are loaded onto trucks destined for the mill. Once there, the logs are unloaded by heavy machinery to be stacked in piles, called decks, where they are routinely sprayed with water to prevent them from drying out.

When the logs are to be milled, they first must be debarked using giant toothed wheels or high-pressure water, and are cut to final length. A computer uses optical sensors to determine the maximum yield of each sawlog, and calculates the optimum cutting pattern. Once secured to an adjustable carriage, the log is milled.

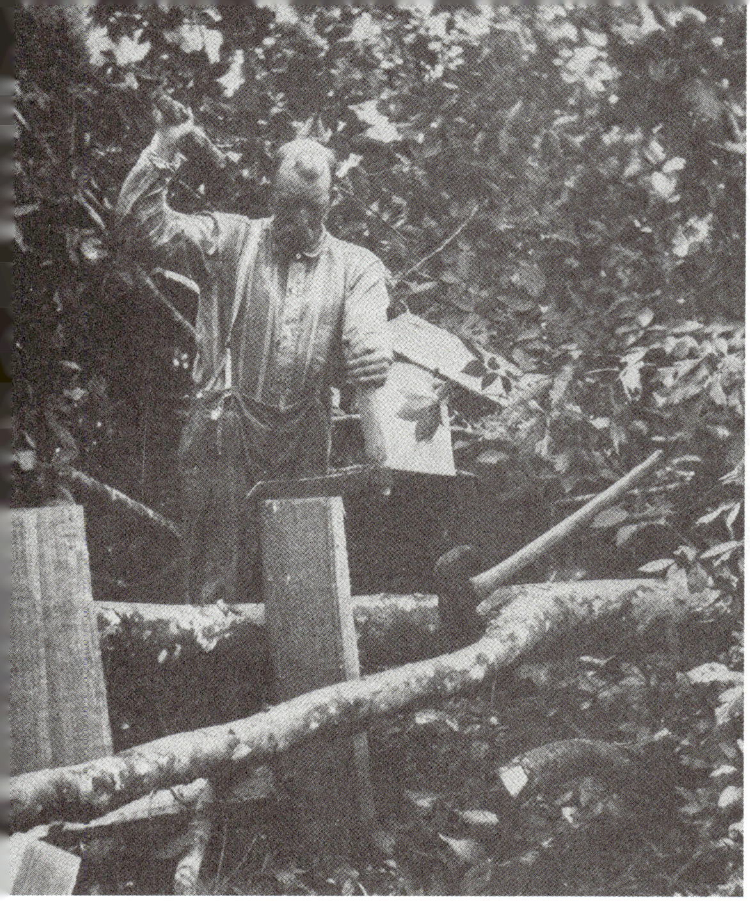
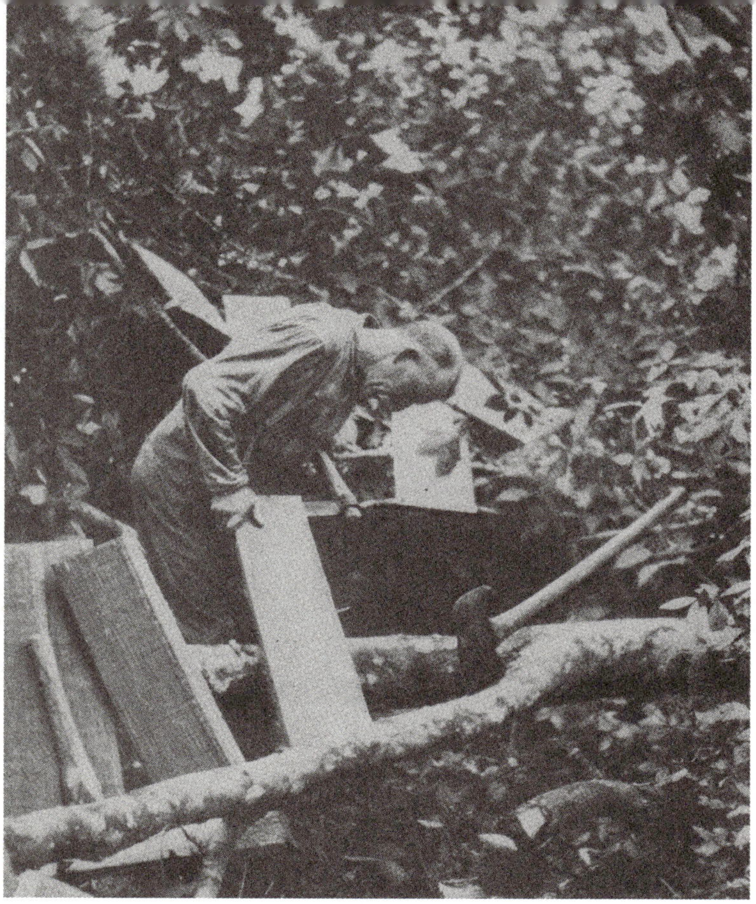
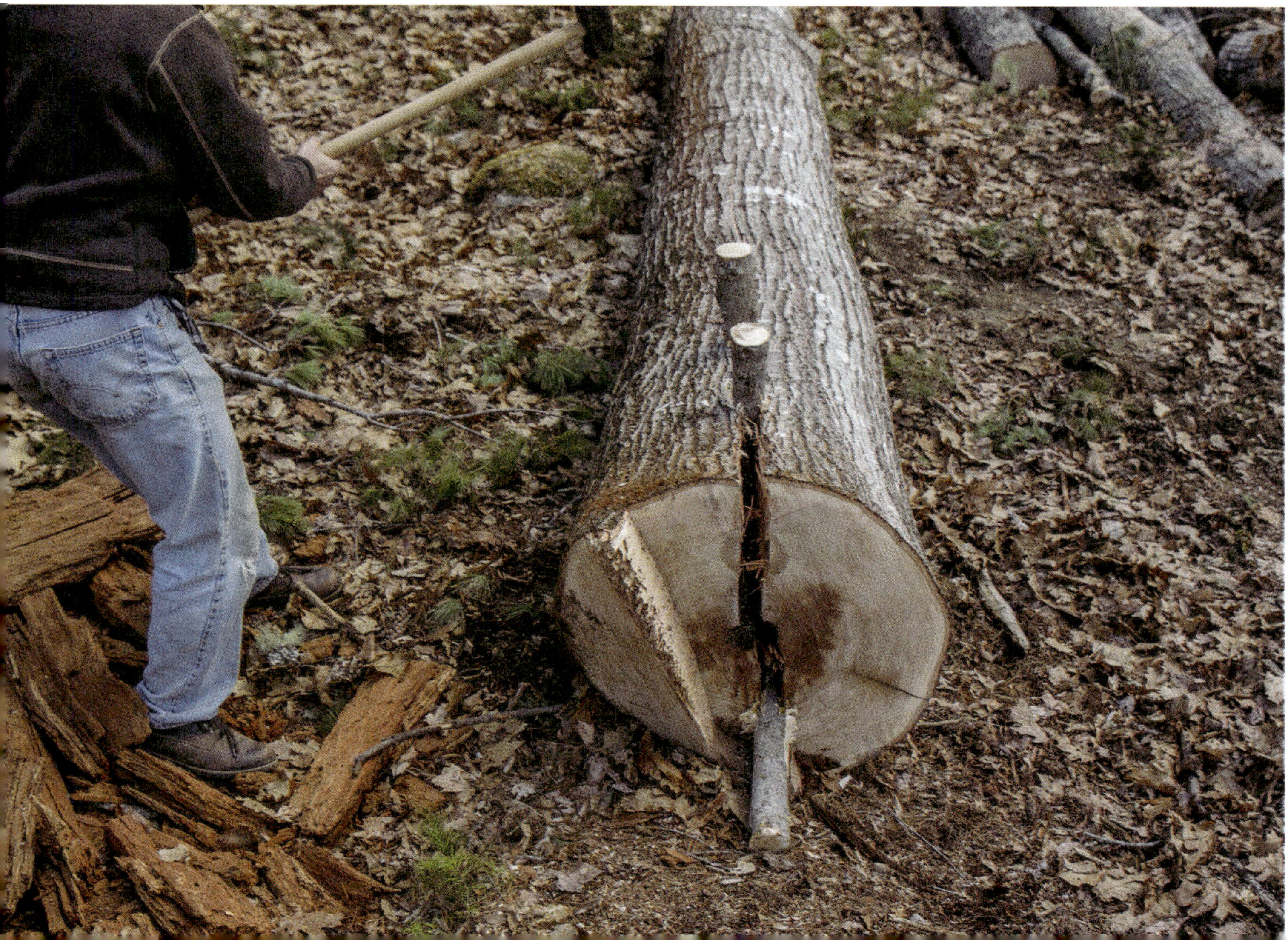

Modern sawmills typically employ vertical bandsaws, though other types are used as well. The resulting slabs from these initial cuts are subject to additional milling to remove wane and produce regular dimensions. Waste wood is usually chipped and discarded or burned.

The rule of thumb for air-drying lumber is one year of drying per inch of thickness, but using a controlled kiln to force the moisture out of milled wood can finish the process in just two to four weeks. Boards are stacked and stickered in an enclosed kiln, where air is heated to temperatures of up to 240°F and circulated through the kiln day and night. Lumber so treated can achieve moisture levels of 6-8 percent, far below the 20 percent typically achieved through air drying.[8] Once this is complete, the finished boards are loaded back onto trucks for transport to distribution hubs. In the case of big-box home centers, a piece of North American lumber might travel thousands of miles before it reaches a local store. Of course, exotics have an even longer trek ahead of them.

This operation, which can potentially begin with a tree that has birds singing in its branches one month and end the following month with a stack of smooth, dry, ready-to-work lumber in a different time zone, seems almost miraculous in its brevity. We truly have reached a pinnacle in harnessing scientific know-how to make an ornery natural material quite tame, approachable, and available. But the process does require a huge input of non-renewable energy, and while going from stump to store so quickly is good for the bottom line, lumber processed in this way can suffer structural damage, case hardening, and cell collapse. Though damage caused by the kiln-drying process is not always visible, it can greatly weaken the material.[9] As wood is a hygroscopic material, constantly varying moisture content in response to changes in ambient humidity, drying it to single-digit moisture levels means that, in most locations, it will have to re-absorb moisture from the air to find equilibrium. We've all seen those corkscrewed 2x4 bananas at the lumberyard that did not respond well to the kiln-drying process – they're not useful for much of anything but kindling.

Beyond the Immediate

When we consider factors such as efficiency and cost, it's important to think about the big picture. To illustrate this, let's look at something near and dear to my heart – food. Regarding immediate cost, the cheapest way to eat a square meal (in terms of calories per dollar) is to hit a fast-food joint.[10] Elaborate supply chains, inexpensive ingredients (made so by the use of genetic modifications and advanced pesticides to support monoculture, government subsidies, and vast factory farms), and a finely honed preparation process make the drive-thru fast, efficient, and easy on the wallet. I simply could not make my own double cheeseburger at home for a dollar, or anywhere near it. But assessing value in terms of immediate cost doesn't take into account the long-term health effects I'm likely to suffer, and pay for financially, on a fast-food diet. Even more, we have to wonder: What is the impact to our society of moving agricultural efforts more and more to subsidized, modified crops with the aim of making them as cheap as possible, or of the massive non-renewable energy expenditure needed to keep the supply network functioning? There are always bigger questions to ask.

So how does this apply to woodworking? Just as cost ought to be considered in broader terms than money spent, efficiency in craft is more than simply how fast something can be produced. We have two pervasive caricatures thrown at us today: one is embodied in those time-lapse power-tool videos we might see on social media, in which a project is blitzed through from start to finish in 59 seconds. The second is the quaint black-and-white memories of the country woodworker of the past, patiently hewing away at a timber one shaving at a time from sunup to sundown.

These two images give us a misleading view of what it is to work efficiently, both by overselling the advantages of modern tooling, and by mischaracterizing the steady, physical nature of period craft. I believe that, not only in terms of speed, but in overall energy usage, sustainability, and cost, the big-picture efficiency of working green wood is remarkable – even radical.

The Efficiency of Simple Tools

Simple hand tools are an essential part of the traditional green woodworking equation. For what they manage to do, these tools are pretty amazing in terms of economical energy expenditure. Let's have a quick refresher in junior-high physics: when talking about using energy to do work, we speak in terms of *watts*. Without getting too far into technical definitions, a watt is a measure of energy transferred over time. Your toaster uses about 1,000 watts to brown your bagel; elite cyclists can generate that much power with their legs for just a few minutes before tiring. Our bodies, with all their functions (thinking, walking, tying shoes, putting that bagel in the toaster) use approximately 100 watts over the course of a day – the same amount of energy that light bulb you left on in the basement is consuming.[11] As we let this sink in for a moment, consider that a table saw requires roughly 4,500 watts to come up to speed, and 1,800 watts of continuous power as it runs.[12] Our arms can generate somewhere between 30-60 watts as we saw a board.[13] If it seems like it takes a bit longer to make a long rip cut by hand than it does on your friend's shiny new SawStop, take heart; even accounting for the slower pace of your work, the table saw requires about five times the total energy input to do the same task as you with your old Disston rip saw.

This power has to be produced somewhere. In the case of the table saw, the mechanical energy to rip lumber is generated by turbines spun by a dammed river, by steam generated by burning coal or nuclear fission, or other means. This mechanical energy must be converted to electrical energy, transmitted over miles of maintained lines, stepped down to a safer voltage for residential use, before finally reaching the shop, where the saw's motor turns it back into mechanical energy to spin the blade and cut the board. Think of the work to maintain this grid, the repairs to lines after a storm, the massive effort required to dig coal from the earth or dispose of spent nuclear fuel. But your old Disston is bagel-powered. This is big-picture efficiency.

We have all heard the argument that using hand tools is hard work. While I can certainly agree with that assessment, I have to ask why that's a bad thing. In our culture it is not uncommon for a person to wake up on a cold, rainy morning, warm up the car, drive a few miles to the gym, and spend the next 45 minutes burning energy on expensive equipment – we consider this to be healthy and disciplined. Though this scenario offers the benefit of quantifiable results (calories burned, specific muscle groups targeted, time and pace), it is not a creative process – no beautiful or useful objects are made for all that energy (electrical, caloric, fossil fuel) consumed. Years ago at the local YMCA, our then 2-year-old son happened to look in on a spinning class – rows of people sweating and cranking hard on exercise bikes while being cheered on by their instructor. His innocent but profound remark has always stuck with me: "Daddy, that's so sad. They're not actually going anywhere." Physical exertion to maintain fitness is a good thing, but imagine what could result were some of that energy poured into creative work. We appreciate and respect the amount of time and effort that goes into training for a marathon or for football season, but we look at hard labor after creative ends as drudgery. This seems backward to me.

Another angle to think about when considering the big picture of efficiency and energy footprints: using old tools. The process of manufacturing that new table saw requires an amazing diversity of materials – iron ore for steel, petroleum for plastics, copper for wiring, cerium-doped phosphor for LEDs – all of which require substantial processing and transporting. Hand tools, being far simpler (basically, a bit of steel on a stick) and less resource-intensive, obviously leave a much smaller manufacturing footprint. But even more, ponder the fact that much (if not all) of the atmospheric carbon released in the manufacture of your vintage saw has already been absorbed by trees and stored away as wood – perhaps as part of that board you just ripped. And in terms of cost-efficiency, old tools are by far the best game in town.

Going With the Grain

The materials used in green woodworking are not remotely uniform – not all oaks are created equal, and the quality of the wood can vary wildly even within an individual tree. Tree selection is critical, and in the past many traditions and superstitions developed around felling – from the proper seasons and phases of the moon to cut timber for specific applications, to the direction the tree is dropped based on seasonal trends of wind and weather. If felling occurred at the wrong time, it was believed that the wood might become wormy, crack, or absorb moisture.[14]

Less-than-ideal grain is counterproductive to efficient process, especially because the primary means a green woodworker uses to reduce the dimension of stock along the grain is *riving*, rather than sawing. Riving, prying the grain apart, is by far the fastest way to accomplish this in clear wood, especially when the lignins and fibers of the wood are green and saturated. The fact that wood is weak along the grain but strong in all other directions can be exploited to great effect for the efficient processing of the log. Wedges, an axe, and a froe are used to rive wood to size, and billets worked in this way have several major advantages over sawn stock. For one, riven wood is much stronger because it follows the grain, whereas sawn lumber can have grain running along, up, down, and through the length of a board. Author Richard Jones states that, "a 25 mm (1") thick riven board is as strong as a sawn board 50 mm (2") thick."[15] Rip-sawn lumber was considered inferior enough that all chairs used by the British government before WWI were required to be fashioned from riven stock, a rule that also applied to tent pegs and rungs on ladders.[16] Steam-bent chair backs, hunting bows, and snowshoes must all be shaped along the grain or spectacular failure is the inevitable result. Naturally bent timbers that follow the grain are much stronger than equivalent sawn pieces, and have been used in shipbuilding and timber structures for thousands of years.

Because the grain of riven wood is continuous from one end to the other, issues of reversing or recalcitrant grain, so common in sawn (especially flatsawn) wood, are generally avoided. The piece is simply worked downhill, from the thicker part to the thinner. This can eliminate a great deal of hair-pulling grain tear-out. Also, riven wood is more rot-resistant, as the long fibers are not compromised to allow water to soak into the wood and cause problems as fences or shingles weather. Roy Underhill notes, "Keep the rough split to the weather at all times in any sort of wood."[17]

"To the woodworker the varied dispositions of woods are almost human: even in the same species they differ, some yielding to his wishes as though glad to co-operate, others stubborn and intractable. The quality of a tree was remembered to the last fragment after the bulk of the log had been used."

– Walter Rose, *The Village Carpenter*

Photo: Dawson Moore.

Working wood wet and using it dry allows easy, efficient shaping of particularly tough woods with simple edge tools. Hickory, our hardest domestic species, shaves like butter when green. This magical virtue of wood is what makes working green stock with hand tools fun and approachable for adults and children alike. Most folks who sit down at a shaving horse for the first time are amazed at the ease with which thick, ribbony peels are generated with the drawknife or spokeshave.

The Efficiency of Using Local Materials

We've already seen how the selection from our local lumberyard has taken a long, circuitous route to reach the racks. As with the local food movement, which seeks to minimize waste by sourcing ingredients nearby, there are real benefits to using wood grown in our own neighborhoods. Dawson Moore, a wood craftsman who lives on a sixth-generation family farm in Michigan, recently procured the raw materials for an entire year's worth of work from a single large birch tree cut on his land. "I got over 1,200 spoons, some hewn bowls, pole-lathe-turned bowls, some cups, and probably some woven bark pieces from that one tree," he says, noting that being able to select a tree that he is personally familiar with greatly aids in his ability to best use materials. "Knots, twists, rot, grain curl, reaction wood will all slow my production process. My hand tools work most efficiently with clear, straight grain." Having this kind of connection with the wood allows Moore freedom from a supply chain that would be unpredictable or difficult to rely upon for his specific needs. "I have full control over the entire process. I always know I have exactly the wood I need, at the time I need it, and that it will have the correct moisture content." But aside from the logistical benefits of harvesting his own wood, Moore notes that there is a vast world of experiential knowledge to be gained.

"It is hard for me to put into words how important this has been to my understanding of how wood behaves materially. You begin to see the potential in a given tree as it stands in the forest. How straight is the trunk? Did it grow in deep shade or at the edge of a field? What's the soil like? Which side of the ridge did it grow on? Was it subjected to high wind? Did it grow fast or slow? Any signs of decay? When you can take all this in and then carve a thousand spoons or whatever from that single tree, you gain a deep understanding of what trees make a good fit for what you do. It's a sort of intuition that develops that I don't think I could gain another way."[18]

If you can't directly source wood from your own land, purchasing unseasoned logs from a firewood supplier can be an inexpensive option. Mike Abbott notes that hardwood planks from a retailer can be 100 times the cost of getting the materials from bought unseasoned logs.[19] I personally keep my eyes peeled as we cycle through our firewood pile each year – there is always some wild-grained maple or beautiful spalted birch begging to be set aside. Other options might include harvesting in public forests that allow woodcutting, contacting local arborists or tree trimmers for leads, or simply cruising the neighborhood after a windstorm and offering to clean up downed trees and limbs for your neighbors. You may even get a few cookies out of the deal.

Historically, craftspeople had to overcome many challenges to secure the wood they needed to produce implements and furniture – many of these difficulties were imposed by the ruling class. Under feudalism in medieval Europe, local lords saw peasants' use of forest resources as a threat to their own security and prosperity, so limits were imposed (and stiff penalties threatened) for the use of timber. Limbs could be gathered "by hook or crook" – whatever could be reached from the ground and either cut with a billhook or broken off with a bent stick.[20] Peasants often viewed such restrictions as infringements on their ancient rights of sharing the forest as common property. Theft of timber from crown land was severely punished with fines, flogging, or imprisonment – if the offenders were caught. There are stories of men going into the forest at night during a blizzard or heavy rain, felling a tree,

Courtesy of Roy Underhill.

"The carpentry of the open countryside ought not to savour too much of the joiner's bench."

– Walter Rose, *The Village Craftsman*

cutting the stump flush to the ground and covering it with moss and debris, then hauling the hulk back to the village, allowing the storm to erase every trace of their work.[21] In New England, the use of the "King's Arrow" blazed into the trunk of the mightiest of pines to proclaim these trees off-limits to everyone but the king for the construction of his sailing ships became a rallying cry for the Revolution, and perhaps inspired the specific targeting of these trees for cutting by locals.[22] Roy Underhill recounts a tale from his "younger, wilder days" when he cut a pile of tipi poles from government land at Cheyenne Mountain, Colorado – the base of NORAD operations.[23] Neither he nor I recommend such gathering practices.

Taking the Workshop to the Woods

Green woodworking is well suited for mobility. The tools are simple and portable, and many aspects of stock prep can be completed right next to the fallen tree. This allows waste products – bark, twigs, rotten areas – to be left to decompose, and only the materials needed must be carried out. The efficiency of woodworking in the forest was not lost on past generations – the bodgers of High Wycombe in England generated countless numbers of turnings and parts for Windsor chair production while working in the beech woods. Pole lathes, shaving horses, and shelters (hovels) were constructed on-site, and the waste generated was burned for warmth or piled around hovels as insulation. Many bodgers stretched their work into the nighttime hours to maximize their wages, securing candles to their lathe poppets to continue turning in the dark.[24] This kind of work persisted right up into the 20th century.

It is simply great fun to work in the woods. Whether whittling while leaning against a tree, riving chair parts, or hewing a bowl on a stump, working outdoors as often as possible adds a new element of enjoyment to woodworking.

Courtesy of Wycombe Museum, High Wycombe, England.

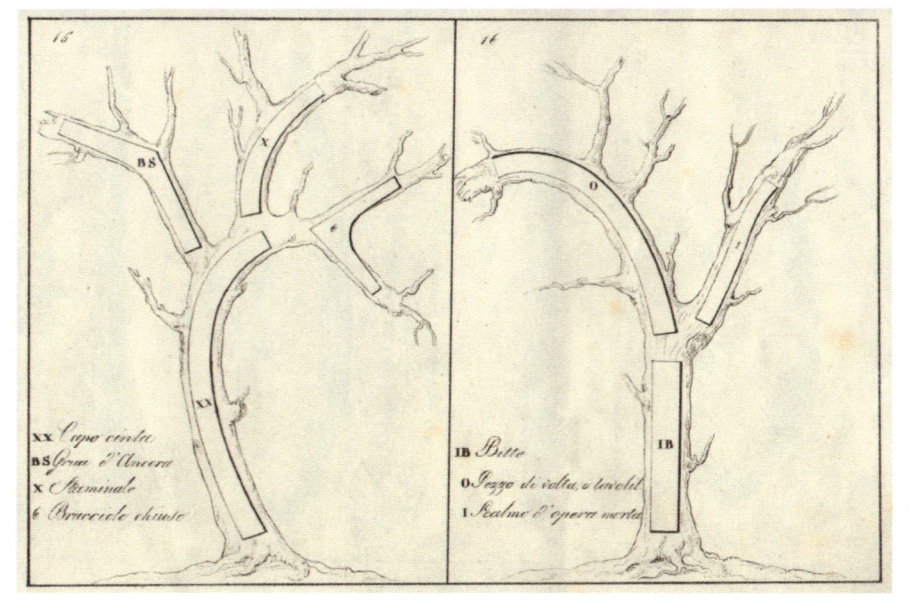

From *Figure de Bezzi di Legname di Costruzione*. Sig. L. Traversa, circa 1820.
Courtesy of Brendan Gaffney.

Letting the Trees Do the Work

Chairmakers, shipwrights, and timber framers need more than straight pieces of wood – they also need curved sections for arm rests and chair backs, bent knees for breasthooks and ribs, and arched timbers to support overhead beams. We might steam-bend these smaller parts (a task for which green wood is ideal), saw them out, or laminate them from many layers of wood and adhesive, but the common historical practice was to seek the needed shapes and curves already grown in the forest. The same grain that runs continuously through straight riven stock also runs through curved branches, knees, and crooked roots. These pieces are exceedingly strong and stable when dry, with the added advantage that the primary work of shaping has already been accomplished. Oftentimes, a branch or limb naturally takes the shape of a specific tool or part, requiring little more than peeling and trimming to put into use.

Using the natural tendencies of trees to increase the production of useful raw materials stretches back to prehistoric times. Many species of trees will send out new shoots from the main stump if the tree comes down due to natural causes such as beaver activity or windstorms. These shoots have the advantage of a massive, mature root system to draw from, and can grow explosively. Coppicing, the art of utilizing this trait for repeated, regular cutting, has been practiced by humankind for many thousands of years. Emmet Van Driesche, a farmer and spoon carver in western Massachusetts, manages a woodlot that produces coppiced Christmas trees, deciduous poles that he uses to create scythe handles, and willow wands for basketry. He notes several key advantages to this method. "There are no seedlings to plant, and the stumps are much more drought-tolerant as their large root systems mean the young sprouts always have access to water." While the process of rotation and multiyear cutting cycles may seem complicated, Van Driesche doesn't feel that way. "All in all, I have found coppicing to be something that people overthink. Coppicing just happens, it is all around us without our realizing it, and it is a low input, low overhead way of producing raw materials again and again." Whereas felling a big tree gives a lot of immediate excitement, coppicing is a quieter method that requires time and patience. "Instead of the immediate object, you focus on the process and on the ecosystem, and on the rhythm of each year and the work that goes into working with that landscape."[25] It is this working with the landscape that sets these processes apart.

Courtesy of Old Sturbridge Village. 2.160.17, Frame Saw.

What we call green woodworking today carried no such particular distinction in the past. Vernacular woodcraft began in the forest, and made great use of the metamorphosing properties of wood as it changes from soft and saturated to hard and dry. Most everything a typical household needed, from treen to transportation, was produced through this process. Nowadays, much of that intimacy with this raw material has been lost as modern woodworkers turn to machines that rely on tame wood and massive infrastructure to function properly.

But trees are not tame, and require knowledge and patience to work in the old way. There are valuable returns for the effort, not just in terms of fulfillment for the individual maker, but in the bigger pictures of sustainability and self-reliance. The tools for the work – axe, froe, drawknife – have remained unchanged for centuries, powered solely by human energy, but there is no end to the creative avenues that can be explored with them.

And who knows? In so doing, you might just help save the world. ◆

ENDNOTES

1. Mike Abbott, *Green Woodwork: Working With Wood the Natural Way* (Lewes, East Sussex: Guild of Master Craftsman Publications, 1989), 15.
2. Ibid.
3. Ants Viires, *Woodworking in Estonia*, trans. Mart Aru (Fort Mitchell, KY: Lost Art Press, 2016), 6.
4. Roy Underhill, *The Woodwright's Guide: Working Wood with Wedge & Edge* (Chapel Hill, NC: The University of North Carolina Press, 2008), 14.
5. William Coperthwaite, *A Handmade Life: In Search of Simplicity* (White River Junction, VT: Chelsea Green Publishing Company, 2007), 2-16.
6. Drew Langsner, *Green Woodworking: Handcrafting Wood from Log to Finished Product* (Emmaus, PA: Rodale Press, 1987), 1.
7. John Alexander, *Make a Chair from a Tree: An Introduction to Working Green Wood* (Newtown, CT: The Taunton Press, Inc., 1978), 12.
8. "How Lumber Is Made," http://www.madehow.com/Volume-3/Lumber.html (accessed 11/23/18).
9. William T. Simpson, Ed., *Dry Kiln Operator's Manual* (U.S. Department of Agriculture, Forest Service, 1991), Chapter 8, https://www.fpl.fs.fed.us/documnts/usda/ah188/chapter08.pdf.
10. Kyle Smith, "The Greatest Food In Human History," *New York Post*, July 28, 2013, https://nypost.com/2013/07/28/the-greatest-food-in-human-history/.
11. Wei Liang Mok, "Power of a Human," *The Physics Factbook*, 2003, https://hypertextbook.com/facts/2003/WeiLiangMok.shtml.
12. "Wattage Estimation Guide," American Honda Motor Co. Inc., https://powerequipment.honda.com/generators/generator-wattage-estimation-guide (accessed 11/19/18).
13. Charles Q. Choi, "The Body Electric," *Knowable Magazine*, April 6, 2018, https://www.knowablemagazine.org/article/technology/2018/body-electric.
14. Viires, *Woodworking in Estonia*, 13-16.
15. Richard Jones, *Cut & Dried: A Woodworker's Guide to Timber Technology* (Fort Mitchell, KY: Lost Art Press, 2018), 8.
16. Abbott, *Green Woodwork*, 23.
17. Roy Underhill, *The Woodwright's Companion: Exploring Traditional Woodcraft* (Chapel Hill, NC: The University of North Carolina Press, 1983), 154.
18. Dawson Moore, email correspondence with author, November, 2018.
19. Abbott, *Green Woodwork*, 21.
20. Underhill, *Companion*, 13.
21. Viires, *Woodworking in Estonia*, 17-18, 243-244.
22. Tom Wessels, *Reading the Forested Landscape: A Natural History of New England* (Woodstock, VT: Countryman Press, 1997), 72-73.
23. Underhill, *Companion*, 7-8.
24. L.J. Mayes, *The History of Chairmaking in High Wycombe* (London: Routledge & Kegan Paul, 1960), 9.
25. Emmet Van Driesche, email correspondence with author, November 17, 2018.

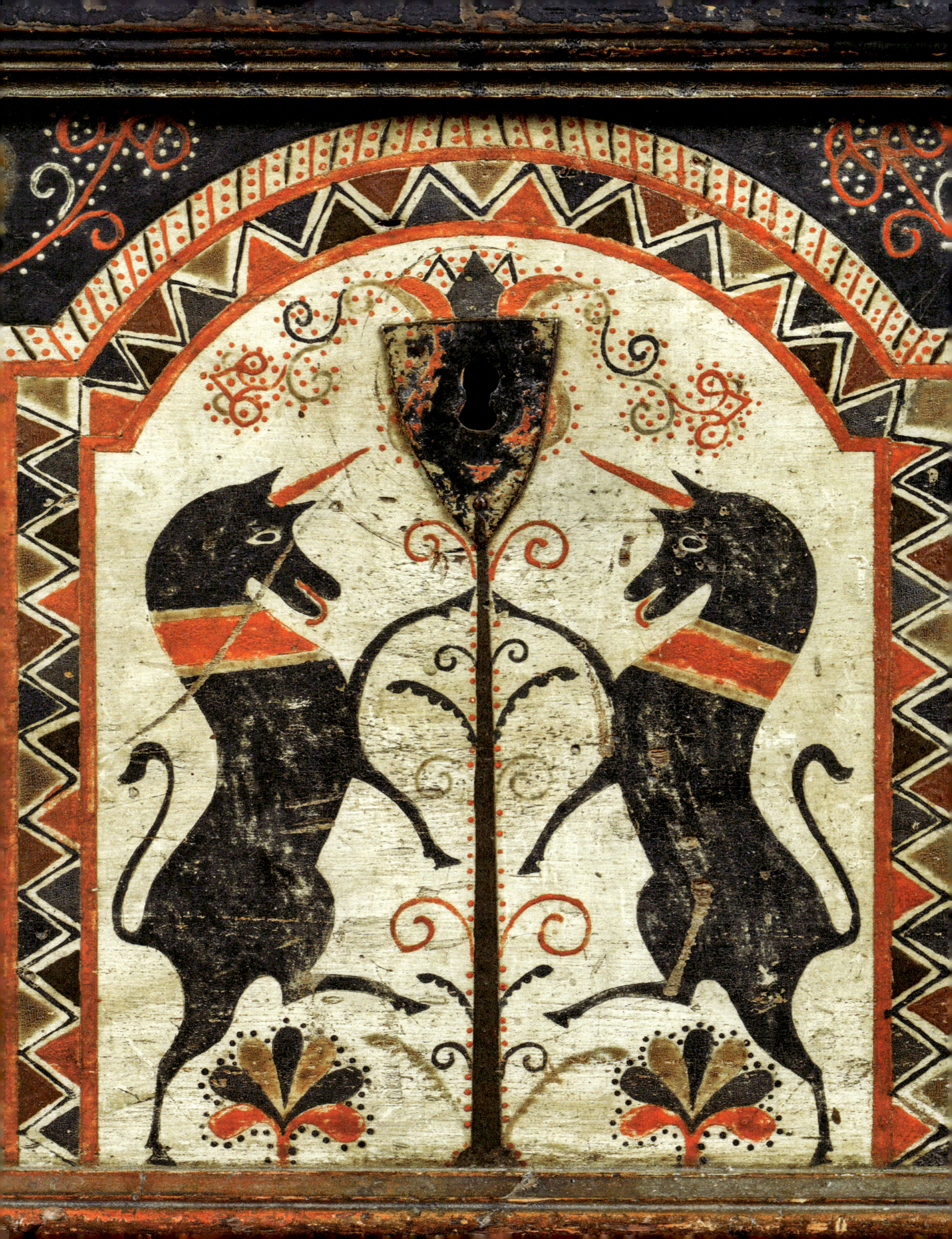

Courtesy of American Folk Art Museum / Art Resource, NY.

A PAINTED CHEST
IN THE
PENNSYLVANIA-GERMAN TRADITION

Jim McConnell

Kannscht du Deitsch Schwetze?

Things have a way of getting lost in translation. The Pennsylvania Dutch, for instance, are Dutch in name alone, and Deutsche (German) in every other respect. Originating from the Rhineland and Lower Palatinate region of Germany and Switzerland, they were displaced by political and economic strife early in the 18th century and sought refuge in North America. These days, one is most likely to encounter the remnants of Pennsylvania-German culture in America through quaint and folksy "hex" signs painted on barns and sold as decoration at tourist shops along rural roadsides, but these too are something of a missed translation – the modern commercial fringes of an elaborate cultural tapestry.

Germanic peoples began arriving in what is now Pennsylvania as early as the late 17th century during the time of William Penn. Though the Pennsylvania Dutch are most often associated with the Amish (often referred to as the "plain Dutch"), among them were also many Lutheran, Reformed, Moravian, Mennonite, Hutterite, and even Catholic faithful. Historian Earl Robacker points out that "many of them were desperately poor, and few were affluent enough to bring more possessions than their sea chests would accommodate."[1]

Dower Chest. ca.1780 Berks County, Pennsylvania. 23.16 Detail.
Courtesy of The Metropolitan Museum of Art.

Dower Chest, ca.1780 Berks County, Pennsylvania. 23.16
Courtesy of The Metropolitan Museum of Art.

As native German speakers, they often had difficulty communicating and integrating with other colonists, and historical narrative suggests that they were so roundly mistreated and despised by the English and Scotch-Irish settlers that they formed intensely insular communities for protection and support. It is these close-knit communities that we have to thank for the preservation of many of the traditions carried over from Europe, and there are perhaps few traditions more fully "Deutsche" than the painted furniture.

Monroe Fabian traces the painted decorations on Pennsylvania-German furniture all the way back to the German and Swiss chests of the late Middle Ages and a time when lower classes began to embellish furniture to emulate the elaborate decorative furniture in wealthier households. Pointing specifically to Upper Bavaria, sometime in the early 17th century, Fabian notes that furniture makers began to decorate "with a rather cautious use of stenciled patterns in black on natural wood."[2] This trend blossomed and had fully developed by the early 18th century when individuals and families from this region began migrating to North America. Painted chests were common and, being eminently useful storage solutions, the chests often migrated as well.[3] Though this article focuses on the Pennsylvania Dutch tradition of painted furniture, it should be said that the migration of these Germanic peoples also extended north through New York, west to Ohio and Indiana, and south through the Shenandoah Valley of Virginia and the piedmont of North Carolina, and the tradition of painted furniture followed there as well.

A Most Practical Art

The two most common forms of painted furniture found in Pennsylvania-German households were the storage chest (*kischt*) and the wardrobe (*shonk*). While wardrobes were very large and almost always used as communal furniture within the home, chests were prized as private pieces of furniture, usually holding the few treasures accumulated over a lifetime. Often, these chests were given as gifts to young men and women to hold their belongings. For young girls, especially, these chests would have been filled with clothes, quilts, and other fabrics to be taken along to their new homes following marriage.[4]

Although these articles of furniture were intended to be practical, when we find them today they are also so wildly embellished with themes of flowers, stars, mermaids, unicorns, and pomegranates that it is hard not to find a certain delight in them. Any blank surface was fair game, and wardrobes and chests often, but not always, bear some sort of identifying information about either the maker or the owner. While this evidence can be helpful in tracing provenance and grouping furniture together, I find this sort of information interesting primarily because it helps me to imagine those who lived around these artifacts. These chests are truly the furniture of necessity, made by jack-of-all-trades country craftsmen for their families and friends, and embellished with love in ways that spur the imagination. It is also evident that they were crafted and decorated in a style that reminded them of their homeland and transcended their isolation, connecting them to the larger *freindschaft* of kin they had left behind.

Dower Chest. ca.1700-1800 Berks County, Pennsylvania. 34.100.2
Courtesy of The Metropolitan Museum of Art.

Construction

Unlike other vernacular chests of the day, extant examples of these Germanic decorated chests suggest that the Pennsylvania Dutch universally eschewed the nailed rabbets favored by the English, preferring dovetailed corners (tails on the front and back boards and pins on the sides) and applied molding around the lid and base. Lids and sides were often single boards when wide stock was available, and if feet were applied, this was done as part of a plinth or bracket base spanning the length of the front and sides, joined with dovetails at the corners. In a point of similarity with English joined chests, a small till was often added with a lid that, when lifted, would serve to prop the top of the chest open. Occasionally, these chests are found with a rank of drawers below the large storage compartment.

The average overall size for a Pennsylvania Dutch decorated chest without drawers is in the neighborhood of 24" tall x 48" long x 22" deep, and soft woods were generally preferred as material for building these chests. Tulip poplar (*Liriodendron tulipifera*) was a favorite because of the clear wide boards available to country cabinetmakers. Although cherry (*Prunus serotina*) and eastern black walnut (*Juglans nigra*) were easily accessible to German immigrants in Pennsylvania, they were used far less frequently.[5]

Defining Characteristics

Part of the unique joy of these chests is their variety, and while there is no typical example, there are certainly common traits that place them unmistakably within this tradition. Pennsylvania Dutch chests can easily be spotted by their use of symmetry, pattern, whimsy, and color.

Of all the defining characteristics of Germanic painted furniture in America, symmetry seems the most universal, with a strong bilateral symmetry exhibited in nearly every example I have seen. Sometimes this is created through painting false "panels" on the front and sides to be filled with other designs, but more often the symmetry is in the design itself. Horses often face each other as if divided by a mirror. Flowers and stars are bisected and plotted equally across a wide surface. Corner designs serve as bookends, wrapping around the edges creating a feeling of balance and completion.

Blanket chest by Johannes Spitler, 1800–1807, Page Co., Virginia. Yellow pine and paint; HOA: 28", WOA: 49-1/2", DOA: 22-3/8". Collection of the Museum of Early Southern Decorative Arts (MESDA) at Old Salem, Acc. 3806, Mrs. Bahnson Gray Purchase Fund.

The idea of pattern also seems to have been very important to furniture decorators in this tradition, but pattern more akin to a quilt pattern than a stencil. Just as certain quilt patterns and motifs have local variation but ultimately can be traced back through the Pennsylvania-German line, there seem to have been general trends in the types of elements included in painted furniture designs, and even similarities in the ways these patterns were executed. This is particularly true of geometric patterns, such as stars, circle flowers, and hearts, but is also evident in the more freehand elements such as tulips and vines. Each artist certainly added their own distinctive touch while working within a clearly identifiable tradition of ideas. Some motifs seem to predate even 16th-century Germany, pointing much further back to ancient Mesopotamia and Persia.[6]

Interestingly enough, given the consistency of patterns in this genre, Fabian points out that "the use of stencils is hardly ever observed on Pennsylvania German chests in the 18th and early 19th centuries."[7] He cites one early decorator who used them to create crisp outlines for painted astragal-end "panels" on the front of his chests, but it wasn't until several decades into the 19th century that the frequent use of stenciling overtook freehand painting as a time-saving measure.

Also, let it never be said that the Pennsylvania Dutch lacked for imagination. Painted furniture in the German-American tradition bears evidence of a deep craving for liveliness, mythology, and whimsy. As Fabian suggests, these chests "exhibit a full range of celestial and earthly subjects" with stars, flowers, hearts, horses, and peacocks right beside more fanciful creatures like unicorns, angels, and the elusive mermaid. Even the common house cat makes an occasional appearance.

The decorators of these chests clearly wanted to incorporate the fullness of life in their work, though the intent of individual decorators in applying particular motifs is sometimes unclear. Fabian suggests that while there is much conjecture about these themes, "almost never are we given any clue by the painter himself." There are clues within the verbal tradition and culture that help make sense of some of the motifs: In Germanic *volkskunde* (folklore), for instance, mermaids are associated with birth (because that's where babies come from), and while modern science has yet to discover a proper species of unicorn, to the 16th-century German mind they were still a distinct possibility. Men with drinking vessels and women with flowers may suggest domesticity or hospitality. A horse and rider began to appear in the historical record symbolizing freedom and rebellion as the American War of Independence approached.

Above all, these chests are colorful. Depending on location, a relatively wide palette of colors was available to artists in the 18th century. Prussian blue, yellow ochre, burnt umber, verdigris (blue-green), Spanish brown, lead white and red, and lampblack, among others, were obtainable at druggists in and around the areas of Lancaster and York, Pennsylvania, by the mid-1700s.[8] These colors were used by furniture decorators as well, and regardless of the color chosen, one trend seems

Pennsylvania-German painted chest: Courtesy of Olde Hope Antiques, Inc., New Hope, Pennsylvania.

Dower Chest. ca.1780 Berks County, Pennsylvania. 23.16 Detail. Courtesy of The Metropolitan Museum of Art.

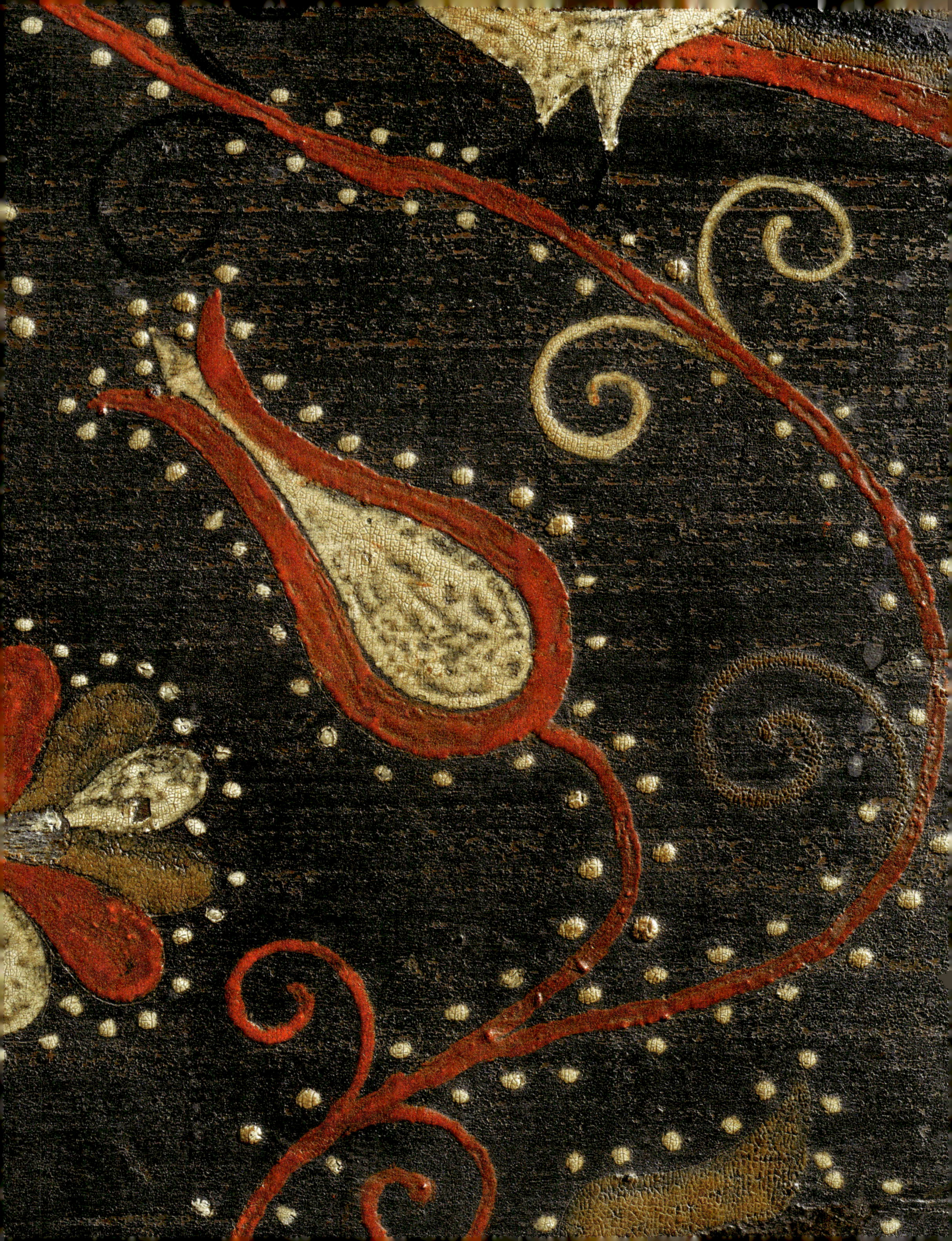

to hold – the brighter, the better. Robacker posits that "unadorned surfaces must have been abhorrent to the Pennsylvania farmers, who made up for their lack of professional achievement in the details of cabinet-making by their thoroughness in applying color, sometimes with garish effect, sometimes with small consideration of proportion, but always with a distinctive touch."[9] While Robacker's assessment of the technical and artistic capacity of these cabinetmakers is overly reductive, his reaction is a good reminder that this style, while near and dear to my heart, may not be for everyone.

Anyone Can Do It

These chests were common furniture in nearly every Pennsylvania-German household in the 18th century, and as such they were as often as not made and decorated by the very families who used them. Growing up around Pennsylvania-Dutch culture and artifacts, I have been eager to understand and indulge in the creative impulses that mark this tradition, and in order to unlock the secrets of these designs I decided to try painting a few patterns myself on a small chest I built for my daughter. The chest itself is much smaller than any historic examples would have been, but it served as a good canvas for a few sample patterns, each of which exemplify the use of color, pattern, symmetry, and whimsy that mark this tradition. Let's begin with color.

Many of these chests were painted with multiple layers of color so I chose deep blue with a red undercoat – a very typical color scheme for 18th-century German-American furniture. I used milk paint for these coats, which would have been available at the time, although some examples exhibit oil-based undercoats. The detail work on these chests was typically done with local or imported pigments with oil or sometimes egg yolk (tempera) as a vehicle. Typical colors for detail work were Prussian blue, yellow ochre, various available reds, lampblack, and lead white, all of which would have been available to varying degree in early 18th-century Pennsylvania.[10]

Perhaps the best lesson to take from this lack of uniformity in medium is that furniture makers weren't overly picky in this regard. They used whatever was on hand because they had no premonition that they would need to meet the standard of historical consistency 300 years later. In that same spirit, after oiling the base coats with boiled linseed oil to seal and enhance the milk paint I decided to paint in the detail and designs with acrylic paints. Artist's oil paints are a good choice if you have time to let them dry, or tempera if you have a few extra eggs in the refrigerator. I happened to be working on a deadline with a very impatient three-year-old customer to satisfy, so the quick-drying properties of acrylic chalk paint fit the bill. Under a sealing coat of wax, it's difficult to tell the difference.

Historically, if these chests were to be decorated in anything more elaborate than plain paint or faux wood texturing, decorators preferred to plot guidelines, designs, and sometimes even detailed motifs on the bare wood. Of the many patterns that appear on these chests, scribed stars, "plump" hearts, and tulips are easily the most common motifs. They're also fairly simple to plot out using a straightedge and compass.

Let's begin with the six-pointed scribed star, often referred to as a "hex" pattern.[11] Start by finding the very center of the lid panel, disregarding the trim. Place one point of your compass on the center point, decide upon a radius by eye, and scribe a circle around the center. Without resetting your compass, place one point at the very top of the circle (measure if you wish to be exact) and scribe an interior arc. Picking up the first point, scribe another arc pivoting from where the previous arc ended. Continue this process around the circle and watch the flower emerge. A similar process can be used to plot a nautical star.

While the scribed star design is geometrically based on the circle, the heart is laid out by first plotting the four outer points of a square. If the heart is to be centered on the finished piece, make sure the square is bisected by the central lateral line of the design. After plotting the four corners, use a compass to lay out the rounded heart tops as three-quarter circles centered on the top two corners. Switch pivot points to the bottom corners and lay out the point of the heart as the inverse continuation of the upper curves. On more elaborate examples of Germanic painted furniture, these hearts are embellished with interior designs such as flowers or stars. Also note that hearts are not always simply hearts. They are often incorporated into more intricate patterns, and an upside-down heart makes the perfect "bulb" for the tulips blooming above.

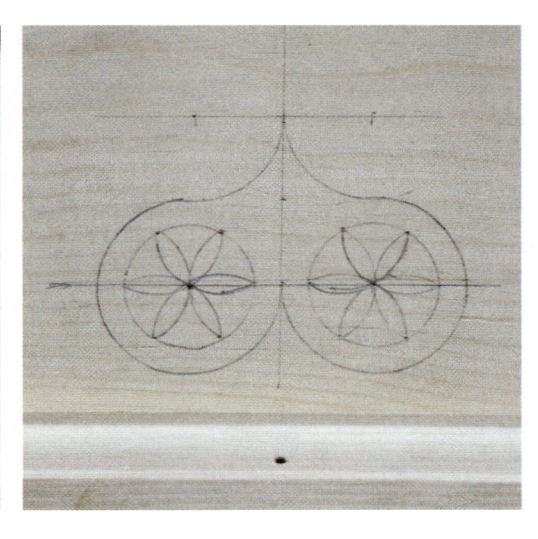

Hearts wrapping around chest corners can be plotted by drawing a single line in from the corner on either face. Beginning roughly 1/4" from the base molding, scribe half hearts with a compass set to the distance between the line and the corner. The larger this distance is, the larger the heart, and vice-versa. I found 1/2" to be a good starting point for well-proportioned hearts.

While tulips are prevalent as a thematic element on many German-American chests, they display great stylistic variety ranging from stenciled precision to flowing and freehand, and for this reason, they are an excellent example of how the artistic styles of these chests diverge while working within a motif. Bilateral symmetry is almost always present in flowering tulips, with one prominent flower in the center flanked by equal numbers of flowers or buds on either side. The flowers themselves may be realistic or quite stylized and the stems display the style and creativity of the decorator.

I began my experiments with the tulip motif trying to uncover a geometric pattern for the flowers and stems similar to the one used to scribe the hearts and flowers described above. I got close, but each attempt left something to be desired. To me, they felt too stiff, and while there are plenty of historic examples with very stylized and geometrical tulips, I found myself favoring the looser freehand style. Perhaps the evident variety in this signature motif comes down to nothing more than personal preference. I scribed the tulips and stems with an awl, taking care to preserve overall visual symmetry but not worrying too much about exactness.

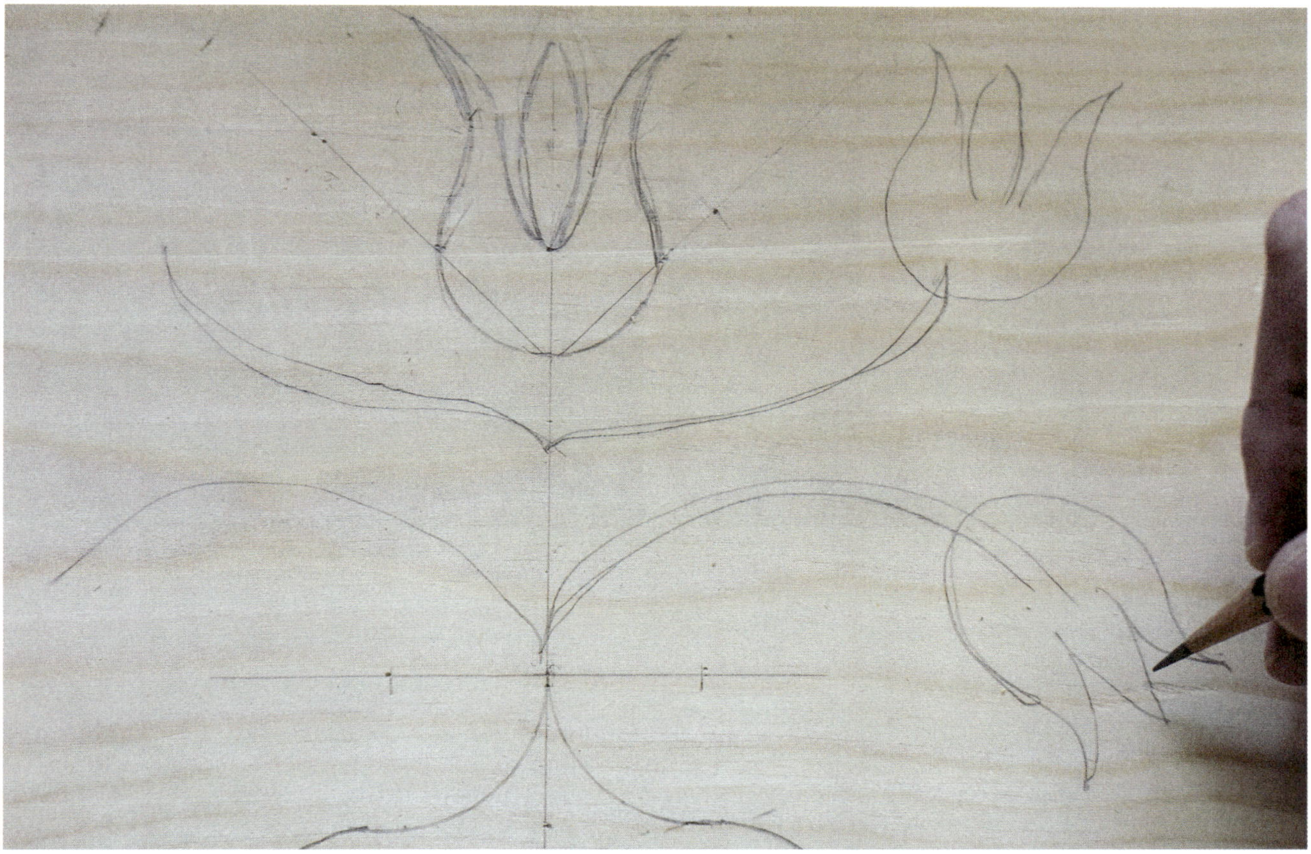

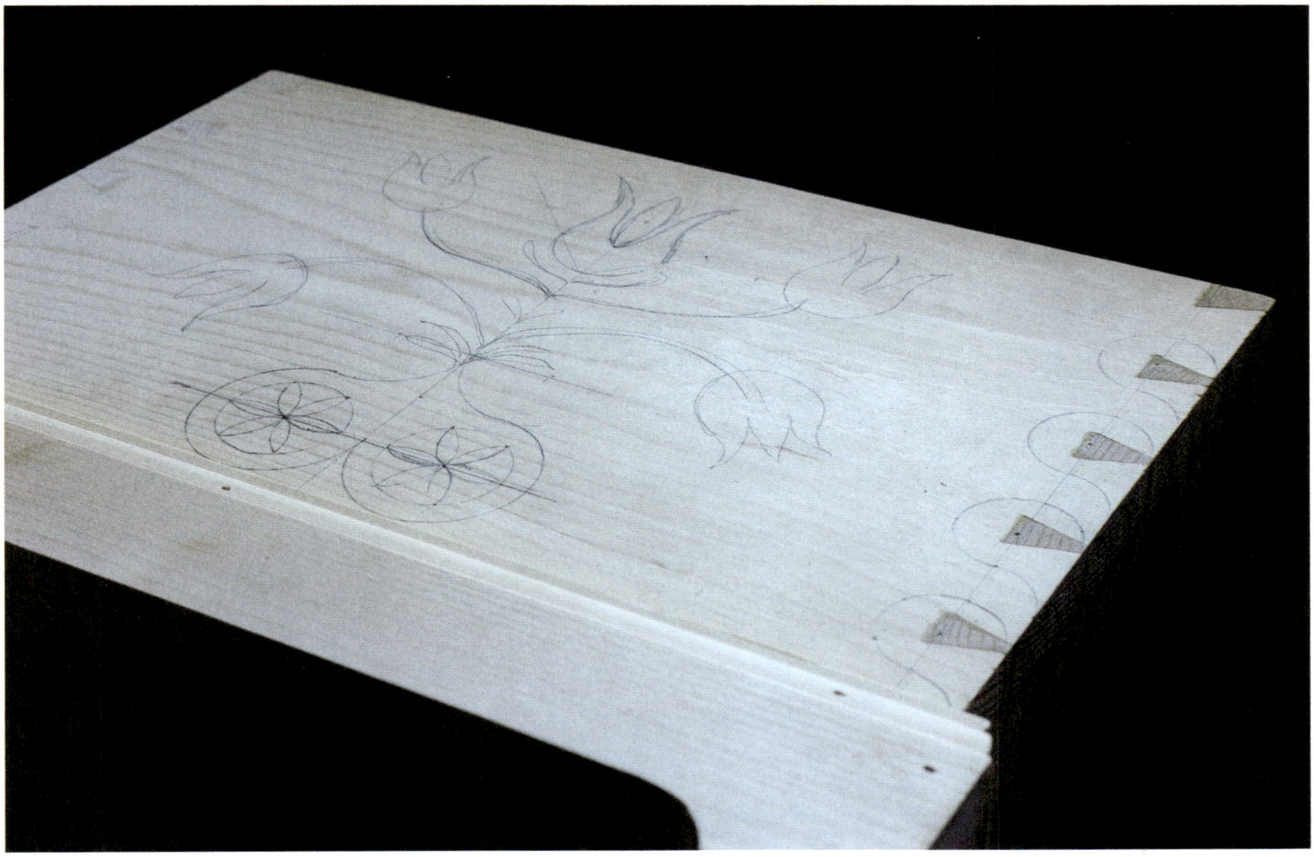

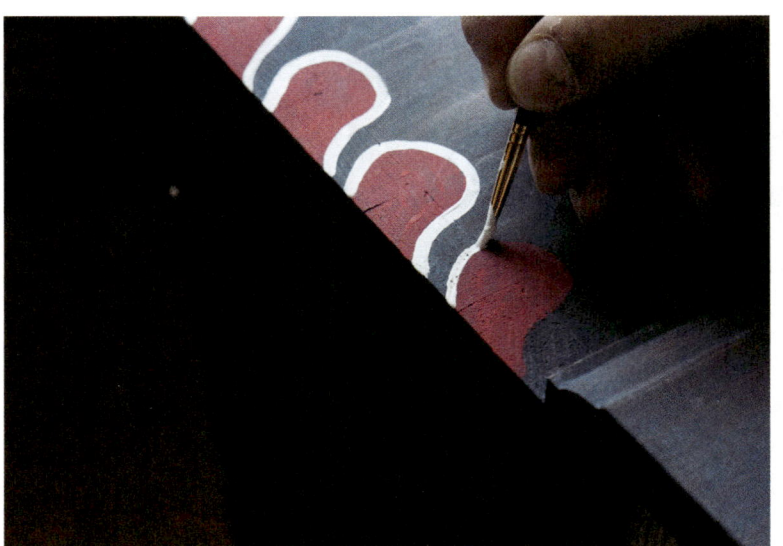

Finishing Touches

Although the designs were scribed into the wood before painting, there were some moments in decorating a chest in this style where I felt like I was working without a net. No open surface on these chests is safe from embellishment, and there are opportunities to exercise great freedom in adding detail. Corollary to that, there are also a host of mistakes waiting to happen and errant brush strokes that must be coaxed into unplanned artistic flourish. Looking at the finished product, I know where my mistakes were, but if you don't tell, I won't. A little dot here and a trailing leaf there can be exercised to great effect, but in the end, the hardest part is knowing when to say "leave it be" and put the paintbrush down.

For those cabinetmakers who made a living producing these chests commercially, a certain style, whether sparse or crowded, becomes evident across the body of their work. For me, the stopping point came when my daughter saw the chest and a look of joy spread across her face. As the vast majority of these chests were made as gifts for friends or family members, I suspect this would have been the stopping point for many of my forebears as well. It's also a good reminder about why these chests exist in the first place; bringing a functional joy into everyday life is something we all can do. ◆

ENDNOTES

1. Earl Robacker, *Pennsylvania Dutch Stuff* (Philadelphia: University of Pennsylvania Press, 1944), 4.
2. Monroe Fabian, *The Pennsylvania-German Painted Chest* (New York: Universe Books, 1978), 17.
3. Ibid., 17-18.
4. Ibid., 28.
5. Ibid., 38.
6. Robacker, *Pennsylvania Dutch Stuff*, 7.
7. Fabian, *The Pennsylvania German Decorated Chest*, 63.
8. Ibid., 53.
9. Robacker, *Pennsylvania Dutch Stuff*, 6.
10. Fabian, *The Pennsylvania-German Painted Chest*, 52.
11. The German word for six, *sechs*, sounded like "hex" to the English neighbors of the Pennsylvania Dutch. The name was attributed to all manner of colorful patterns and the custom of calling these "hex signs" persists today.

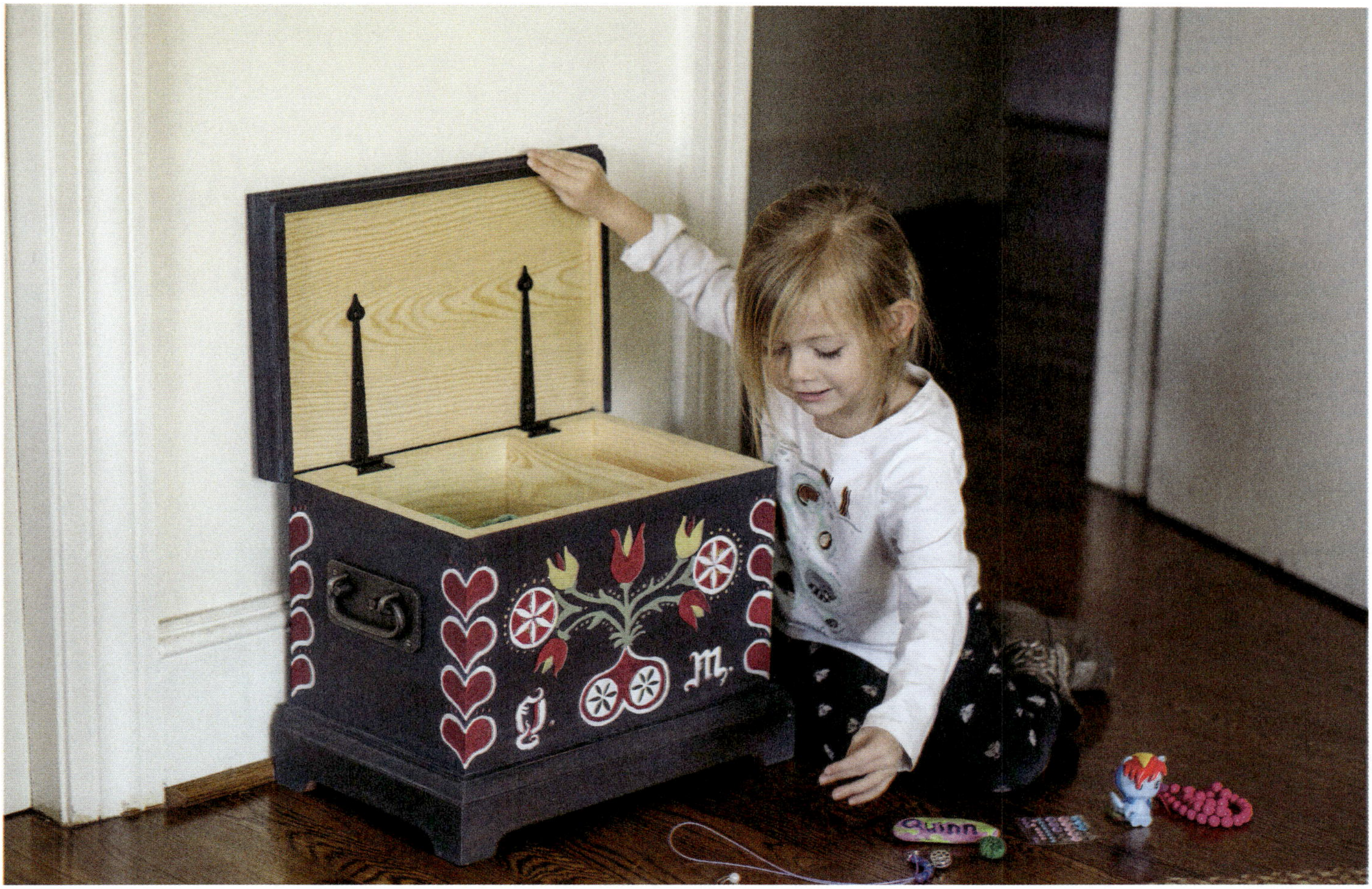

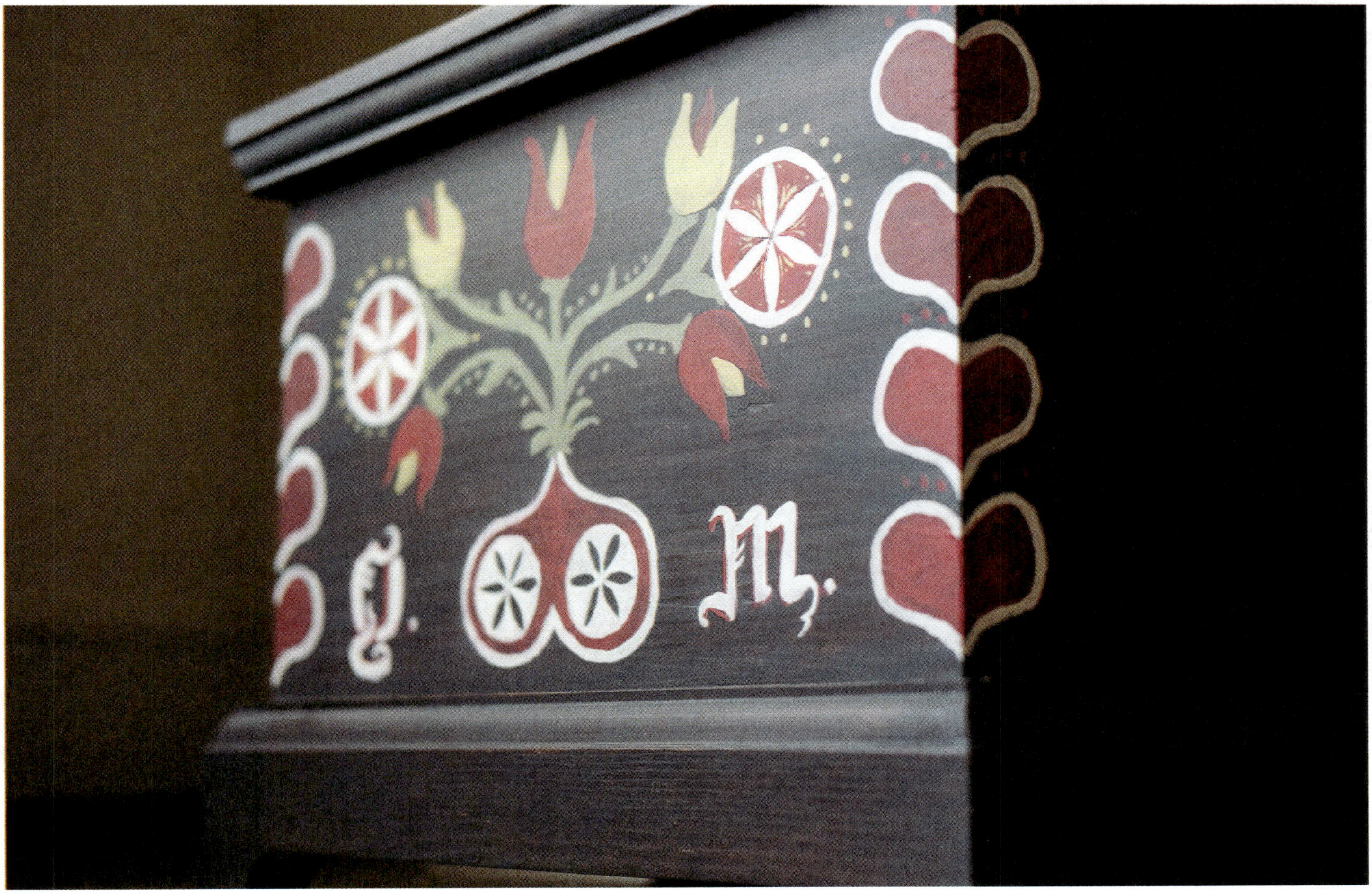

THE WOODEN BRACE
Bitstock Technology for the 21st Century

Joshua A. Klein

"What makes it difficult for the average man to be a universalist is that the average man has to be a specialist; he has not only to learn one trade but to learn it so well as to uphold him in a more or less ruthless society."

– G. K. Chesterton[1]

We live in a society dependent on specialization. Recently, the cooktop on my range started acting funny – one front burner heated slowly and the other didn't come on until it was set at nearly full blast. Then the "Burner Hot" light wouldn't turn off. When we called our appliance repair guy and described the symptoms, he was confident it would be a simple fix. After some digging into the switches and wires, he realized the problem was more complicated than he had thought. But in exchange for a bill for a few hours of head scratching, he finally sorted out our issues – or so we thought. Now, the "Burner Hot" light wouldn't stay on and one of the rear burners was raging hot at every dial setting. Amazingly, after a handful of follow-up visits, a second technician, and several swapped components, the darn thing is finally working right again.

Although the range is an obvious blessing to our family because it enables us to cook our meals efficiently, its complexity leaves me dependent on two trained and experienced technicians for repair.

Because complex modern society is maintained only through specialization, most of us focus our career development in one narrow track. We develop skills in one area in order to get a job to make money to pay other specialists to make and repair our stuff. It is possible in the modern world to become a renowned expert in a particular discipline but be helpless in every other area of life.

But it was not always this way. Before Americans turned to factory work in the 19th century, skilled tradesmen worked for the most part on their own or in small shops that offered diverse goods and services. Especially in rural settings, defining one's occupation was tricky. Was humble Jack a farmer or cabinetmaker or carpenter? Well, yes. All these and more. In the 18th century and earlier, the generalist's diversification of skill was not rooted in a quaint idealization, but in the necessities of rural life.

It shouldn't be surprising, then, that when searching through collections of American pre-industrial tools, many are found to be user-made. Though established English tool-making industries sold their products to the colonial artisans, it was also common practice for American woodworkers to purchase only the plane irons, chisels, and bits, then fabricate the wooden parts to their own liking. Before the Industrial Revolution, it was simply unremarkable to make your own tools. Everyone did.

In our day of hyper-specialization, tool making

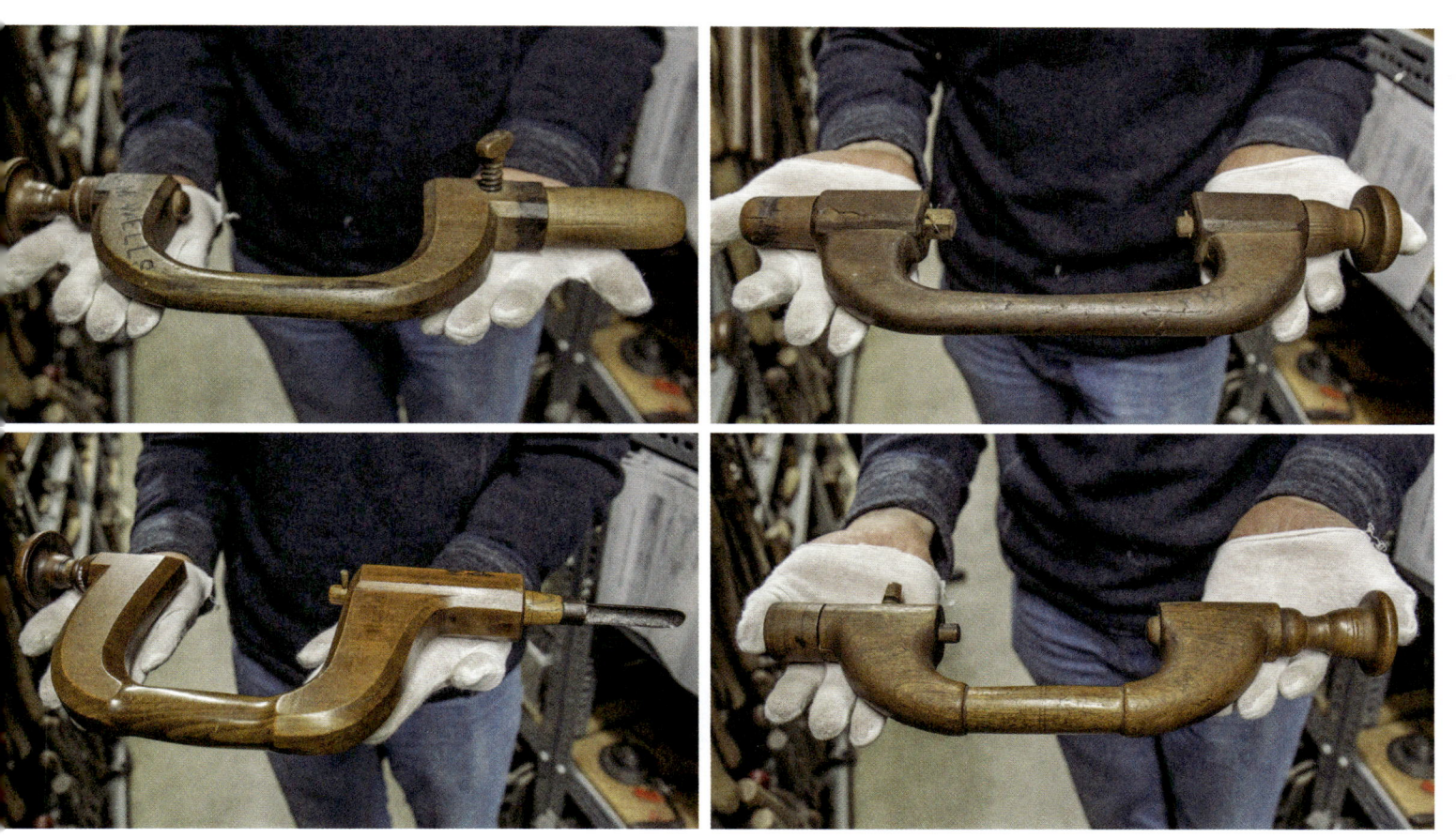

Courtesy of Old Sturbridge Village. 86.44.3a-b, 1.154.34, 1.154.29, and 1.154.42a.

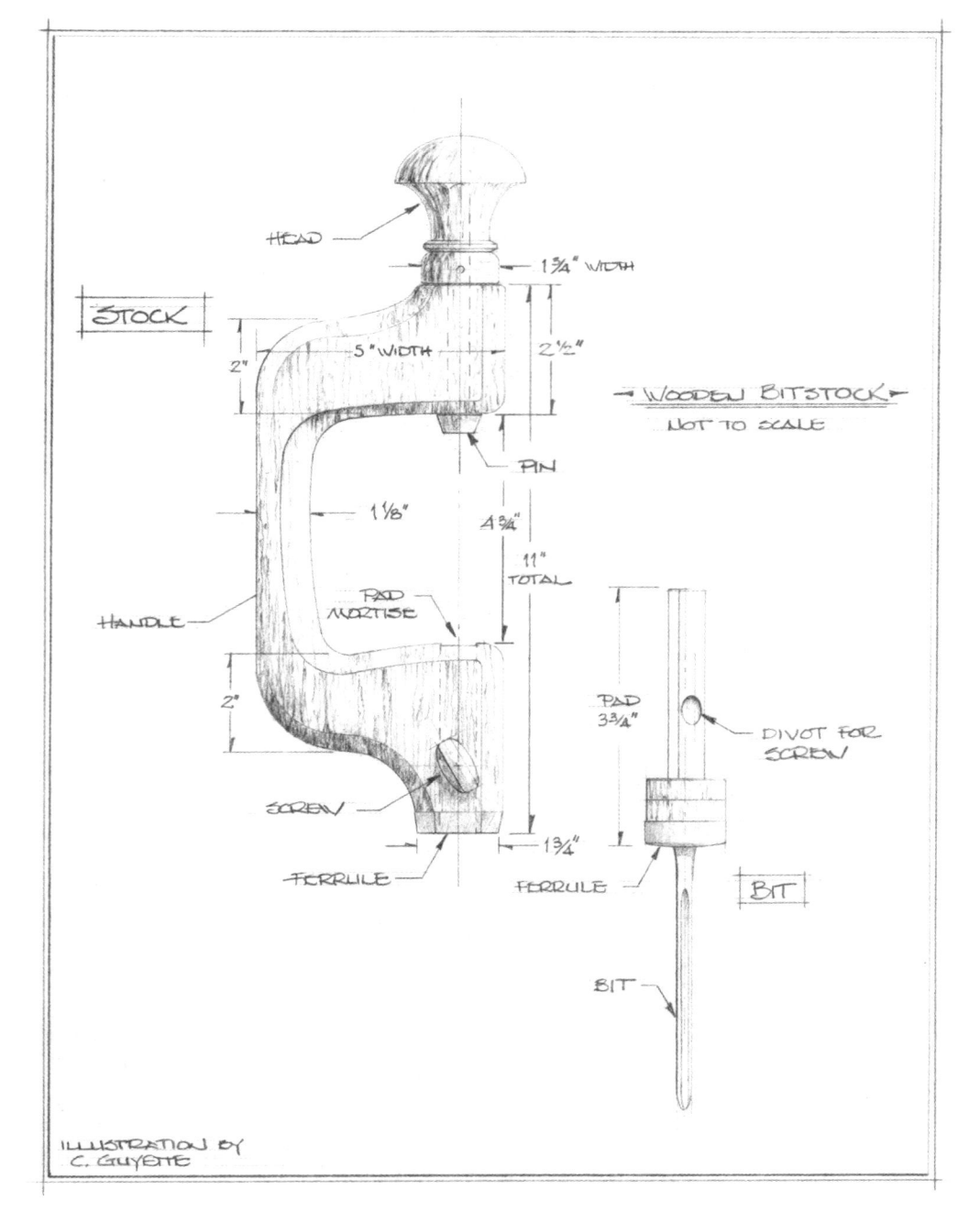

Illustration: Wooden Bitstock (not to scale), showing Stock, Head (1 3/4" width), 5" width, 2", 2 1/2", Pin, Handle, 1 1/8", 4 3/4", 11" total, Pad Mortise, 2", Screw, Ferrule, 1 3/4", Pad 3 3/4", Divot for Screw, Ferrule, Bit. Illustration by C. Guyette.

makes you a more independent craftsperson. Understanding tool dynamics enables you to instantly diagnose, say, a clogged plane throat or a wobbly brace. If you have the ability to adjust, mend, or replace the tool on your own, you are less reliant on the expertise of specialists to fix your problems for you.

In the following, I share my experiments making wooden braces or "bitstocks." Bitstocks were often idiosyncratic tools that reflected the preferences of their makers. A quick image search for antique bitstocks reveals a tremendous diversity in appearance and design. No two are alike.

This project seems simple at first glance, but I had enough dead ends and "back-to-the-drawing-board" moments that I believe sharing them here will be of value to folks who want to try their hand at making their own.

Bitstock History

Variously called a "bitstock," a "wimble," a "brace," and a "breast stock," as well as infinite variations on these terms, this tool has been around in essentially the same form since the beginning of the 15th century. It was first used by housewrights to bore pilot holes for the augers that bored peg holes, which is likely why, in 1678, Joseph Moxon called this tool a "piercer."

Bits were either permanently fit in the brace itself or into interchangeable wooden pads. Later in the 19th century, the springed-button chuck was developed and was offered alongside fancy embellishments such as heavy chamfers and brass plates. Although metal-bodied braces have been around almost as long as their wooden counterparts, they were used for boring into metal, not wood. It wasn't until the 1860s, with the invention of the Spofford split-chuck, followed by the ubiquitous Barber "shell" chuck, that cabinetmakers and joiners began switching over to metal braces.[2]

is often seen as out of reach for the average woodworker. But it is hardly something to fear – a plane is little more than a hole in a block of wood with a wedge, and a brace is nothing more than a curvy stick with a bit at the end. If you can make a table, you can make your own tools.

I still remember the first table I made. After the last coat of finish dried and I stepped back for one final inspection, a feeling of satisfaction overwhelmed me. I was delighted that I had made that table with my own two hands. I couldn't wait to start another project. And thus, my woodworking journey began. I'm sure many of you can relate.

Making your own tools is rewarding in much the same way, but at a deeper level. It teaches you the dynamics at play when a steel edge engages wood in any given tool, which broadens your knowledge base and

The Stock

The stock (or the "body") of my brace was made of 8/4 soft maple for its strength and resistance to the torsional stress induced during boring. Many period bitstocks were less than 1-1/2" thick and the thinnest ones often fractured at short-grain areas. For this reason, split-prone, open-pore woods such as ash or oak were generally avoided.

After truing one edge, I marked out the critical transitions and penciled some freehand curves to get a sense of the final proportions. Once I was pleased with the look, I cut the stock from the plank and sawed relief cuts in toward the handle. But before splitting out the waste, I beveled the handle edge to make a 1-1/8"-thick handle, scribed the bit axis line, and bored the head and pad mortises.

For accuracy's sake, I fastened the stock to the workbench top and bored the two 5/8" mortises for the head and the pads horizontally, guided by a straightedge. Care and accuracy cannot be overemphasized here because ensuring that these holes are true to the axis is the most critical detail of the entire build. Every other step revolves around it.

I recommend practicing this operation on scrap wood a few times before attempting it on your stock. Go slow and check your alignment every few turns. If you have a long bit (such as a T-handled auger) or a bit extension, you could do both mortises from the same direction, using the first hole as a guide for the second. I didn't bother; I just bored from both sides.

With the mortises bored, I split out the waste up to the handle to make it 1-1/8" square. To evenly round it, I planed a series of chamfers, progressing from four faces, to eight, to 16. These facets were then easily faired with the swipe of a spokeshave. At this point, I established the curves and chamfers. I used a knife, chisels, rasps, files, spokeshaves, and a razor blade used as a scraper.

The Head

Almost every antique bitstock I've seen has a head that was turned on a lathe. If you don't have a lathe, you could, of course, carve a head for this project, but I would encourage you to use this opportunity to build a simple spring-pole lathe for your shop – I find mine to be incredibly useful.

The head is joined to the stock with a wooden pin that fits tightly into a hole in the bottom of the head, but is made slightly narrower in the stock mortise so that it spins freely. I selected wood for the head that was slightly above the moisture content of the pin so that the joint would dry together tightly. I waited to permanently affix the head with a wooden pin until the very end of the project because it tended to get in the way during the rest of construction.

The Mortise for the Pads

Before metal chucks were introduced in the 19th century, bits were made interchangeable by fastening them into wooden "pads" that could be secured into a tapered mortise in the stock. Many period bit pads have slightly tapered shafts so that they fit snugly in use, but are easy to remove when needed. Based on the antique examples I've seen, I tapered mine from 3/4" to 5/8" over their 3-3/4" length. Tapering this mortise from the 5/8" hole is a challenge because the work can only be done from the bottom, forcing you to always fight against the grain. Sharp chisels are a good start but small rasps or floats enable you to take it the rest of the way.

The Wooden Screw & the Spring Clip

There are many ways that bit pads are secured into their stocks, including a tight friction fit, a wedge from the top, a wooden screw, a wooden pin, and spring-clip shafts. The simplest method is the friction fit.[3] To make this style of pad, the bit is installed in square stock and the taper planed. The only downside to this system is that the pad tends to become stuck when pressure is exerted during boring. To avoid this, I locked mine in place with a wooden screw.

I used a 1/2" screwbox and tap to make the small screw.[4] Starting with a small piece of maple, I carved a knob and round shaft, checking the final sizing of the shaft in the guide hole of the screwbox. I then twisted the shaft into the box to begin cutting threads. Because the guide plate on my box will not allow me to thread closer than 1" to the knob, I backed the screw out, removed the plate from the box, and finished cutting the threads all the way down to the knob. I then bored and tapped a hole into the stock to receive the screw. Make sure you test different-sized holes with the tap before boring into your brace.

A more complex method of securing the bit into the stock is by a spring-clip shaft.[5] This works by tension, springing into place once the bisected shaft comes up through the top of the mortise. To remove the pad, all that's required is a pinch of the hooks and the shaft can be withdrawn. It is a clever system that can be used if you do not have a screwbox, but the disadvantages are that the shaft is more complicated to lay out and fit, and the labor must be reinvested in every new bit. In contrast, the screw system requires each new pad to receive only a single divot. In fact, making the screw and tapping the hole took me less time than it did to make a single spring-clip pad.

Pads & Bits

If you can get your mind around the subtleties of wooden pads and the installation of their bits, you've got the heart of bitstock making. For this project, I used vintage taper-tanged "shell" bits. These early-style bits resemble out-cannel gouges (pretty much the simplest bit there ever was). If you cannot find these on eBay or at flea markets, you can use others including gimlet, auger, or center bits. I've also made my own shell bits from 1/4" O1 steel rod. They are dead simple: Grind half of the thickness away, form a flute with the edge of an abrasive wheel, give it a 20° bevel, and hammer a flat tang after heating with a MAPP gas torch. Period bits that were intended to be fit into wooden pads had flat tangs like this, but the more common 19th-century square taper-tanged bits can be used without modification.

After trying several approaches, my preferred way to make wooden pads is to do two at a time – I dimension closed-pore hardwood to 1-1/2" x 1-1/2" in about 16" lengths, then knife the primary transitions: the bit end of the pad, the shoulder, and the end of the shaft. To lay out the 3/4" to 5/8" shaft taper, I have a simple template block that is designed to be used with 1-1/2" stock. I scribe this taper on the block from both sides, then do the same on the opposite face before sawing the waste away.

The template can be used again to lay out the next two saw cuts to create the square pyramidal frustum you're after. After sawing, it is a good idea to do any final fitting of the shafts to the stock's mortise before turning and separating the pads. As you pare the shaft and check the fit, make sure you insert the pad in the same orientation every time, because humans don't make perfectly square holes. Aim for a fit that is snug with gentle hand pressure. As soon as the shaft is fit, I trace the screw hole onto the inserted shaft and bore it so that I never wonder about the pad's orientation.

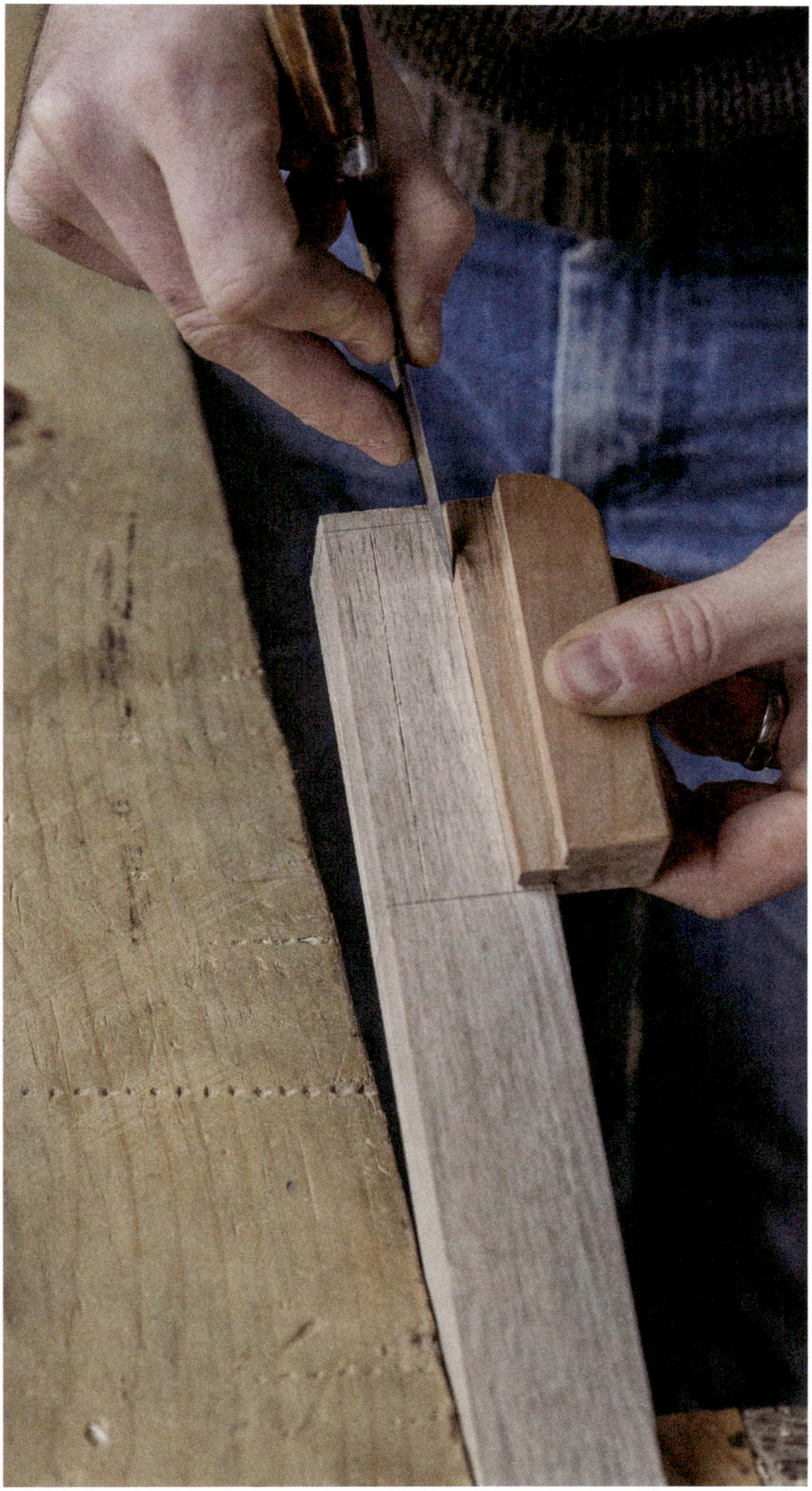
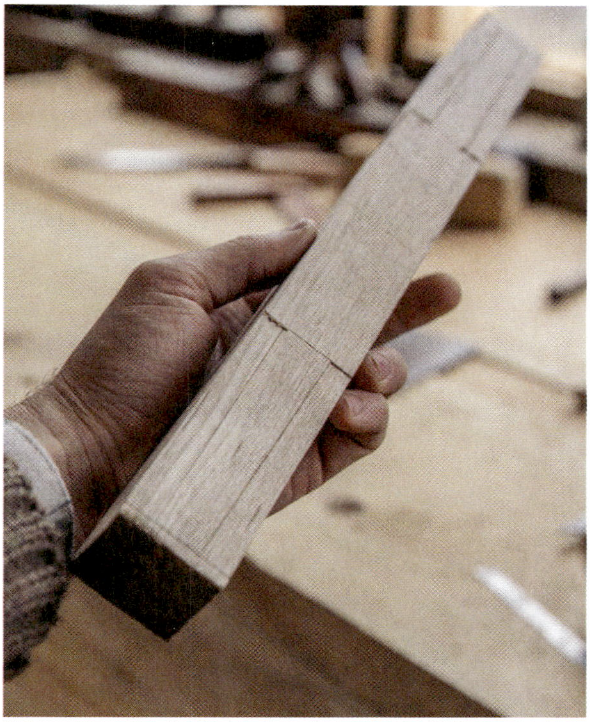
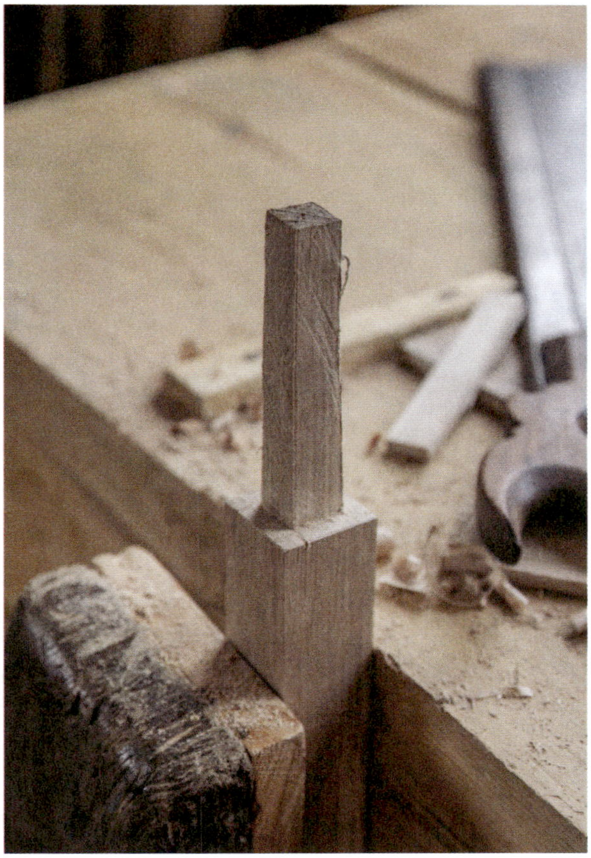

Once the two shafts are fit, I round the pads at my spring-pole lathe and remove material for the pewter ferrule. I reduce the diameter of the end of the pad by 1/8" (for a 1/8" pewter ring) but cut the ferrule shoulder a little deeper. This deeper shoulder produces a tapered column that locks the ring onto the pad were it ever to come loose. I first encountered this technique while studying the pads of Jonathan Fisher, a pre-industrial Maine furniture maker.[6] The pads are separated at the lathe to the smallest dimension possible (just shy of breakage) in order to leave a center mark for the bit installation.

Installing common antique bits into pads is complicated by their tapered tangs. Though earlier bits had flat tangs that made installation easier, I prefer not to irreparably modify antique tools at the grinder. Rather than see the taper as a disadvantage, I have come up with a way to exploit both the shape of the tang and the hygroscopic nature of the wooden pad to make a fit that only comes apart through destruction. To get this fit, I soak the end of the pad in water for an hour before mortising. This swells the wood just enough to ensure that it will shrink down tight onto the bit once in place.

The elephant in the room, however, is how in the world do you reliably bore such a complex-shaped mortise in the end of the pad exactly in line with the stock's axis? The problem with boring and paring these mortises (even if you could do so accurately) is that the nature of the taper forces you to work against the grain 100 percent of the time. This makes fitting a headache. I've bored and pared the mortise several times before, and it's no fun and not predictable.

Instead, I burn the mortises.[7] By heating the tang with a MAPP gas torch, I can plunge the bit into the pad (with it installed in the stock) a little at a time, carefully monitoring squareness with the aid of straightedges. The first time I did this, I laughed out loud. I couldn't believe how easy it was. This process is simple, quick, and dead-on accurate. What more could you ask for?[8]

Here's how I do it: Before heating the bit, I bore a small pilot hole in the pad deeper than the tang because it makes the burning effortless. You can make a mock-up steel tang to do the burning, but if the business end of the bit is wrapped in a damp cloth and the heat application is carefully monitored, there is little risk of ruining the temper of the cutting edge.

Holding the bit with pliers, I apply the flame to the tang, focusing heat on the thickest section. When the very end of the tang begins to show a deep red, I press it into the pad's pilot hole, eyeing the straightedge for accuracy. (It is handy to have a helper sight one of these angles for you, but it can be done alone without too much fuss.) The smoke billowing from the pad as it burns can obscure your vision so doing this in an area with a cross breeze would be ideal. I mortise the bit about 1/8" deeper than the swell of the tang. Once I get to final depth, I remove the tang with as straight a motion as possible in order to leave the final shape unmarred. After the bit is cool, it can be gently tapped into the mortise on the bench. It should be a perfect fit but any necessary adjustments are quick. If it wobbles, try deepening the pilot hole because the bit might just be bottomed. After it's tapped into the mortise tight without wobble, leave it overnight. By morning, the little water remaining should be lost and the bit held firmly.

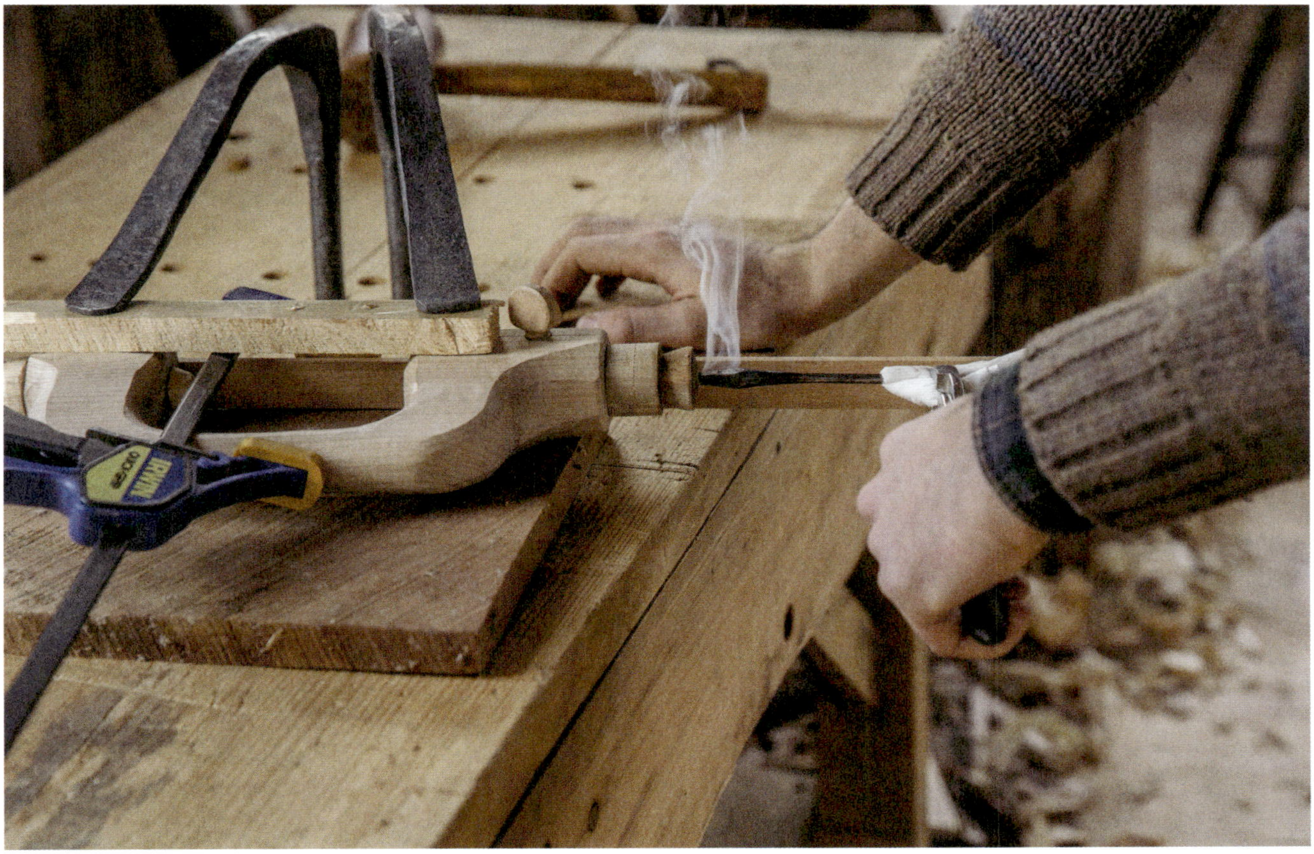
IRWIN

Ferrules

Many period bit pads (and their stocks) were reinforced with metal to prevent splitting in use, typically iron or brass rings, wrapped sheet metal, or cast pewter.[9] Installing ring ferrules is largely a matter of paring the wood and driving the metal to fit. It's a straightforward operation that will be intuitive to any woodworker. But casting pewter was foreign territory to me and I was tempted to try it. Initially, I wondered if it would be a complicated hassle and if my inexperience would produce unsatisfactory results. Did it have too formidable a learning curve? Would it just turn out to be a hare-brained experiment leading me into a dead end? There was only one way to find out.

I prepared the wooden pad by carving a few grooves in the column with a veiner gouge. These grooves key the pewter to prevent the ferrule from spinning. I made a form for the ferrule by wrapping the pad in cardstock and masking tape a little proud of the pad (shown above). When doing this, it's important to make sure the form is tight so that it doesn't leak, and that the form is not distorted because the pewter will fill whatever shape you pour it in. First, I secured the pad vertically in locking pliers on top of a plywood scrap. After hacksawing a chunk of Britannia pewter from the ingot, I melted it directly into a casting ladle.[10] By pointing a MAPP gas torch directly at the pewter, it became 600° molten metal within seconds. (Words to the wise: Don't spill.)

The first time I did this, I didn't know what to expect. To be honest, for all my trepidation and anticipation, the actual pour was surprisingly unremarkable – I tipped the ladle and the metal filled the hole to the brim. Easy as pie. After about 10 minutes, the pewter had cooled, and I faired and smoothed it with files.

Curious about the structural integrity of these ferrules, I cast a 1/8" ring onto the end of a dowel and proceeded to beat the snot out of it. Even after driving a pile of wedge-shaped cut nails deep into the end grain of the dowel, the pewter didn't flinch. Instead, the dowel shattered several inches below the ferrule. Then, I pulled the mess apart and hammered the ferrule by itself – it took considerable abuse to get it to deform noticeably. Based on this simple experiment, I am confident that pewter ferrules are more than sufficient for a bit pad.

Brass or steel ferrules can also be used but they won't have the dovetail-type locking advantage of this casting method, and fitting them is a somewhat meticulous job. Because molten pewter fills all voids, the pad's column can be any random size or shape. Because of this, I believe casting pewter is the fastest, easiest, and most effective of the ferrule options.

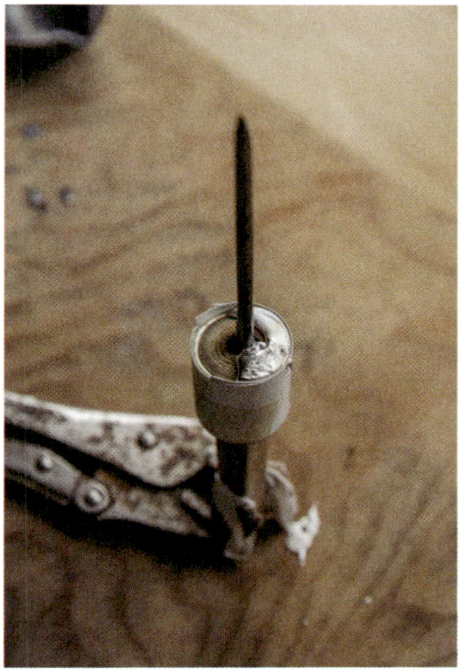

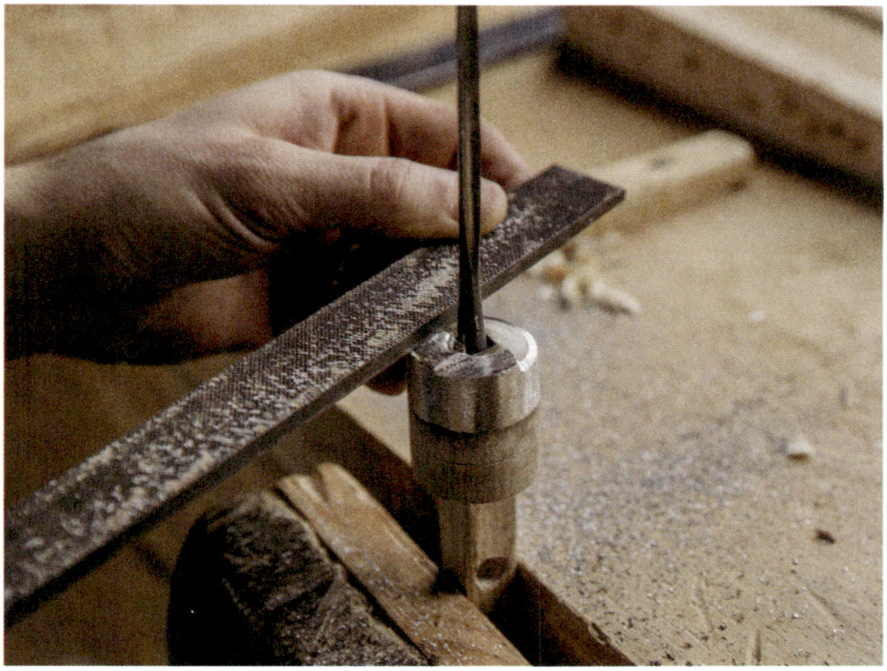

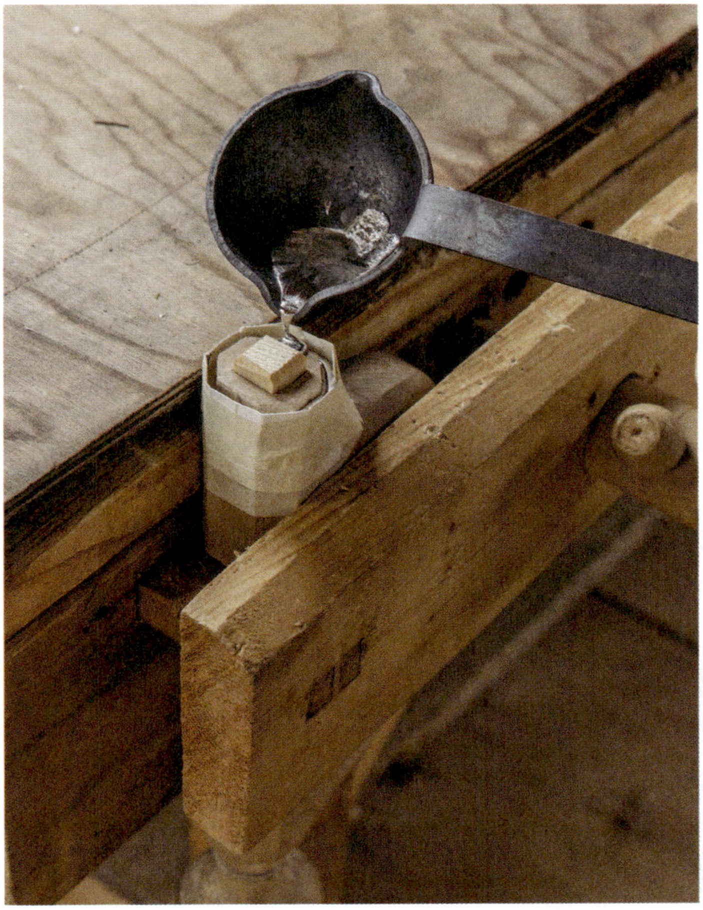

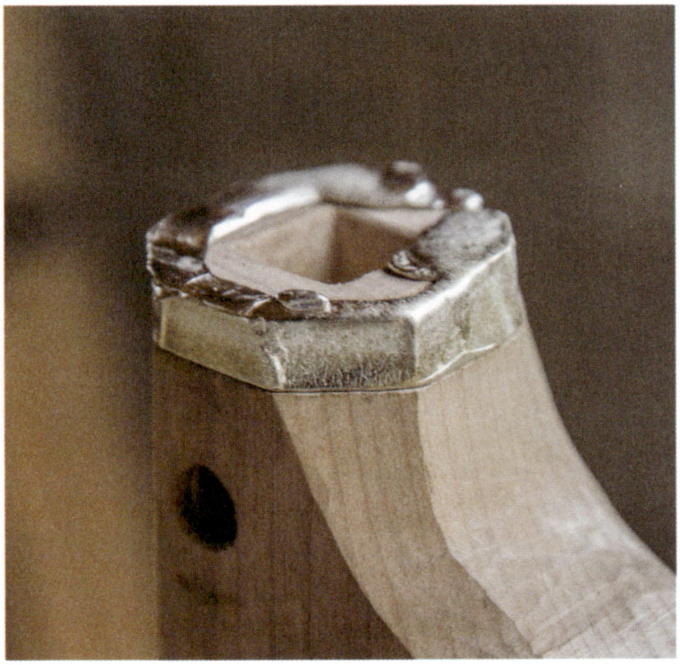

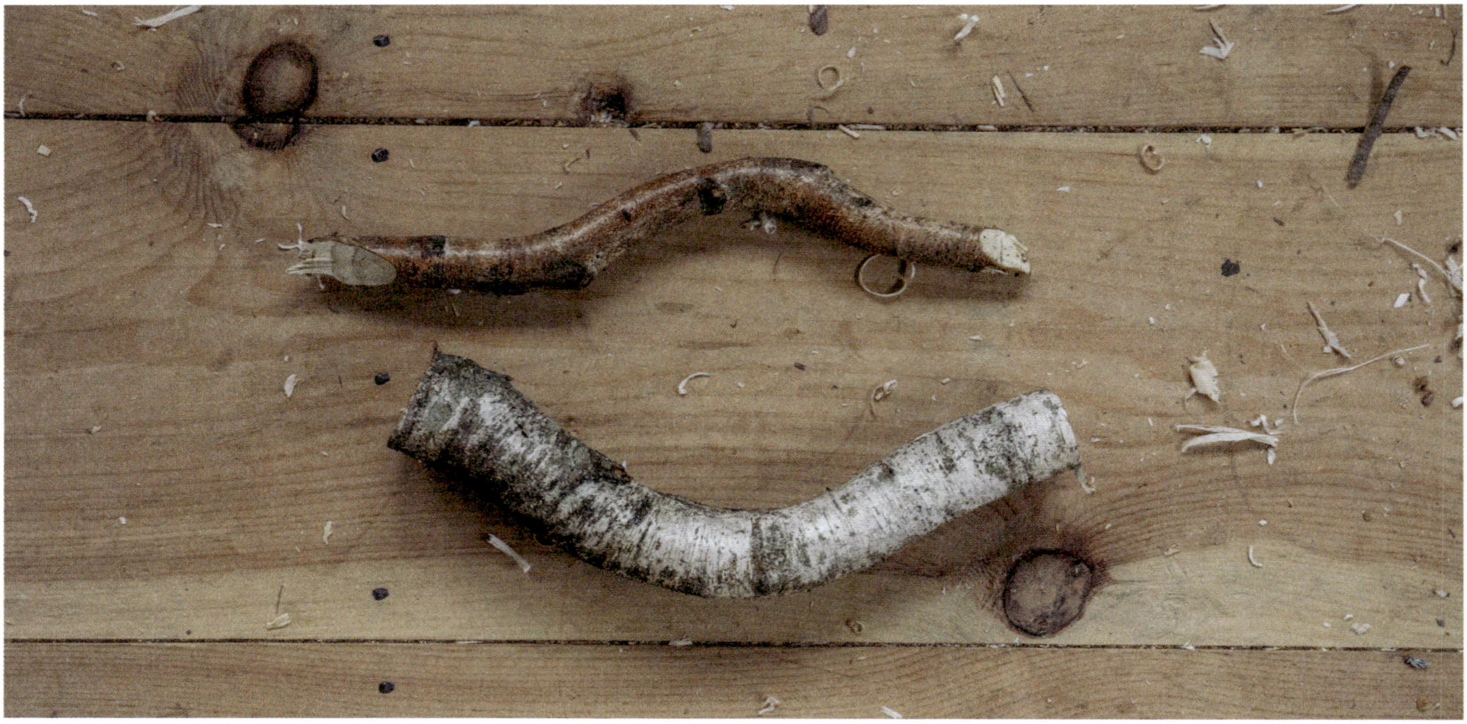

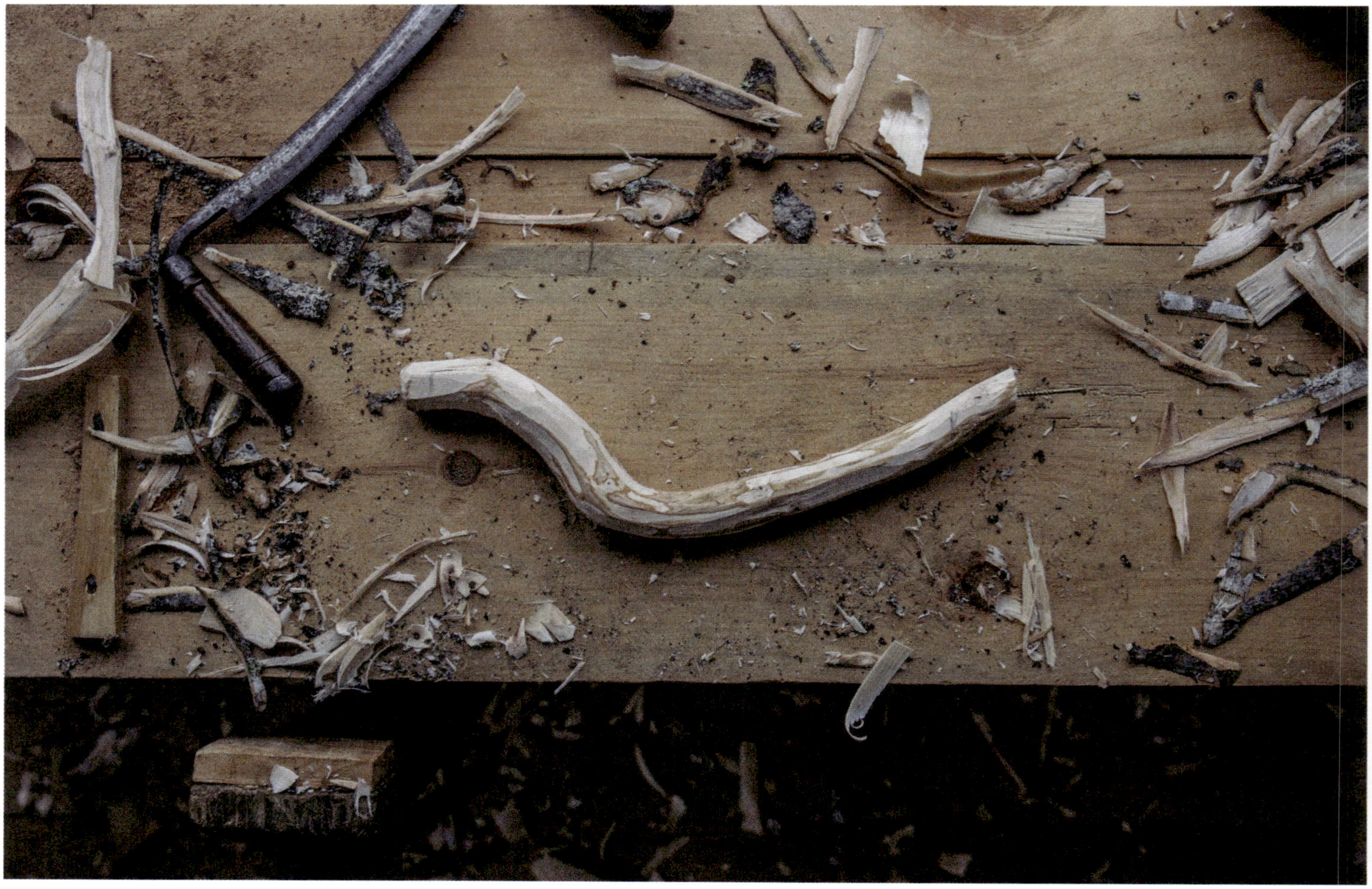

The Crooked Branch Bitstock

One of the historic bitstock ideas that tempted me from the inception of this project was that of using the natural curve of a tree branch to provide the sweep. I learned that this method was relatively uncommon. (Many bitstocks that look at first glance as if they were from a branch elbow were, in fact, sawn from a straight-grained plank.) Because splits at short-grain areas are common, it was hard for me to ignore the advantage of continuous grain on such a serpentine shape. It seemed like this would be the best way to make a brace, and I wondered why relatively few examples of these exist. After making several, I think I have an idea why.

I threw on my pack basket and set out into the forest on a hunt for the perfect branch. Wandering through the woods to find one specific curve was much harder than I thought it would be. I was looking for a sweep of at least 4" that straightened out on either side, but could be no more than 14" in total length. I ended up harvesting three options – all of white birch. Two had a curve that returned straight, and one was a thicker elbow into which I sawed and shaped a handle.

The making of this form is much the same as making one sawn from a plank. The obvious advantage is that much of the shaping is done for you, but the difficulty lies in creating a straight axis because the branch has no flat reference face. I scribed a straight line and bored, guided by a straightedge (as with the plank version), but the result was dissatisfying. The brace wobbles in use. But this is more annoying than dysfunctional – though the wobble makes holes that are slightly conical, in practice, the nails or wooden pins that will be driven into them conform the holes to their shapes anyway. Still, the wobble is awkward and clumsy feeling.

Another aspect of the branch experiment was to see if I would be successful using freshly cut branches. This was an attempt to get around a one- or two-year drying period. I began working the three pieces at different stages of freshness: the same day of cutting, a few weeks of drying, and a few months of drying.

The freshest piece I worked was the elbow stock. I expected it to warp as it dried, but it did so even more than anticipated because, due to the way it grew, it was reaction wood. The other two pieces did not warp as severely. If you're feeling lucky, I would recommend giving branches at least a month or two of drying (without bark on) before boring along the axis. If you want to play it safe, let it dry for a full year.

The complication with boring the axis in a curved branch is that once the lead screw starts to grip into the cross grain of the curve, it veers out for more cross grain seemingly to get a better bite. This forces the hole out of line with the axis. I have tried this over and over and every time I get the same result. It seems using a bit that does not have a lead screw is the only way to go.

As disappointing as it is to report, so far I have not found an easy and successful way to use a curved branch in this application. I had high hopes but have been thwarted over and over. If I weren't so stubborn, I'd give up on this idea all together. But I will continue to experiment.

The "Breast Stock" in Use

Although they can often be seen hanging on shop walls or lying on floors in pre-industrial paintings, I was surprised to find relatively few visual representations of bitstocks, or "breast stocks," as they were often called, in use.

Pre-20th-century textual sources describe the use of the tool with striking consistency. Joseph Moxon, in his description of how to use a T-handled auger, indirectly explains how the bitstock (the "piercer," he calls it) was used: "When you use it, the Stuff you work upon is commonly laid low under you, that you may the easier use your strength upon it....You must bear your strength Perpendicularly straight to the end of the Bitt, as with the Piercer." The anonymous author of the 1839 *The Joiner and Cabinetmaker* describes it much the same: The head "is made smooth and flat, to rest against the chest, that the workman may press hard upon it, and get plenty of power to bore with." Peter Nicholson (1812) also tells us the head is "placed against the breast while boring." Curiously, texts from the end of the 19th century and early 20th century describe and depict the brace used two-handed (one hand on the handle and one on the head).[11] While one might theorize that this is because these texts assume the use of auger bits with self-feeding lead screws, a closer look reveals that shell and center bits were still the most commonly used in that time.[12] My brief survey reveals a pattern: The earliest sources describe the brace as used against the breast to rely on the craftsman's bodyweight, while books written around the turn of the 20th century explain the alternative two-handed method common today. Why this difference exists, I am still trying to figure out.

As I've explored these work positions in my own shop, a few observations bear mentioning. First is that the original breast-held position leaves one hand free to steady the workpiece, which is, in fact, what is shown in early depictions. This enables the artisan to bore efficiently without fixing the piece in a vise.

My second observation is the discomfort of pressing the head firmly against your breast. The period images I've seen show the head pressed against one breast and the handle turned with the opposite hand. This works, but is mighty uncomfortable. I've tried many heads in this position: small, large, flat, domed; they all hurt. I can't help but wonder, "Am I doing something wrong here?" I assume this technique requires a callus much the same way new guitar players' fingers ache until they toughen up over time.

In fact, one source tells us this was the case. Some period chairmakers wore wooden bibs with a central circular hollow to receive the bitstock's head (shown left).[13] Although this was presumably to relieve the pressure from boring, Leonard John Mayes recorded the painful process High Wycombe apprentices experienced as they grew accustomed to their bibs. One "old framer" told Mayes that "the first month or two of using it were often very painful, so much so that sometimes when he got home at night the bib, his shirt and his chest would be stuck together with blood… but…after a month or two your chest hardened and you never noticed the bib again."[14]

So why bother then? What's the advantage of pressing the tool against your body? These sources tell us (and my own experience verifies) that this is for efficiency. Leveraging your body weight onto the bit expedites the boring process.[15] I will continue to explore the use of this tool in different postures to see how I can maximize advantages without going home with a bleeding chest each night. I can say for certain that boring horizontally with the head against my belly is both comfortable and efficient.

Workshop of Robert Campin. Annunciation Triptych (Merode Altarpiece) ca. 1427–32. 56.70a–c Courtesy of The Metropolitan Museum of Art.

Conclusion

The pursuit of independence through making your own tools is a journey full of rewards. The broader a craftsperson's competency, the more successfully he or she will be able to open whole new realms of creative possibility and manage hurdles that come along in the making process. This bitstock project brings together various skills that many furniture makers don't get to exercise often enough: long accurate boring, turning, casting pewter, burning mortises, and utilizing naturally crooked branches.

  Even more, it is a joy to work with tools that reflect your own unique personality and individual aesthetic preferences, something we miss out on if our tool chest is filled with those identical to everyone else's. So I invite you to make your own bitstock, because this project is one more opportunity to engage with time-tested wisdom that empowers you to build your own world. ◆

ENDNOTES

1. G. K. Chesterton, *What's Wrong with the World* (New York: Sheed and Ward, 1956), 92.
2. W. L. Goodman, *The History of Woodworking Tools* (London: G. Bell and Sons, 1976), 179.
3. This style pad was used by the Dominy family and can be seen in Charles Hummel, *With Hammer In Hand* (Charlottesville, VA: The University Press of Virginia, 1968).
4. "Tap and Die Wood Threading Set" from http://garrettwade.com.
5. The earliest example of a spring-clip pad that I have found is in a brace in Stockholm dated 1764. This reference is in Goodman, *The History of Woodworking Tools*, 175.
6. Ironically, I discovered this technique from a pad of Fisher's that had no ferrule, although it appears to have been intended to have one. Due to its unmarred condition and the extreme taper of the column, it seems unlikely that this was ever fitted with one.
7. I do not know of direct evidence of heat-mortising bits into pads, because I suspect that their flat tangs made this technique unnecessary. I developed this technique from period tanged-chisel-making practice, which Willard Anderson and Peter Ross discussed in "Get a Handle on Mortise Chisels" in *Popular Woodworking Magazine*, June 2014.
8. Any reader concerned about the use of the torch indoors should know that it is commonly used in kitchens to sear meat. If you doubt the safety of your own circumstances, it doesn't hurt to do this operation outdoors.
9. "Worked upon stock for a breast bit….Worked upon my bit stock. Went to Major Day's and Uncle Fisher's. Cast a ferrel [sic] for my bit stock." Jonathan Fisher, Diary, September 4th and 5th, 1798.
10. This lead-free pewter is "Alloy AC Casting Pewter Ingot (92% Tin,7.75% Sb,0.25% Cu) Britannia - 563F - 650F" (SKU: PewterACBritannia) at http://rotometals.com.
11. One such example is the comment in David Denning, *The Art and Craft of Cabinet-Making* (Bath: Sir Isaac Pitman & Sons, 1891), 139: "One hand turns the brace while the other presses on the knob on top, though occasionally it is more convenient to place this against the worker's chest. In this position the base is kept more steady while being turned."
12. Otto Salomon, *Teacher's Hand-Book of Slöjd* (Boston, New York, Chicago: Silver Burdett & Co., 1891), 110.
13. In French chairmaking shops, the bib was so standard that their stocks didn't even have heads -- they had small conical points that fit into holes in the bib.
14. L.J. Mayes, *The History of Chairmaking in High Wycombe* (London: Routledge & Kegan Paul, 1960), 13-14.
15. (Insert pun about "expediting boring work" here.)

The CABINETMAKER'S SHOP

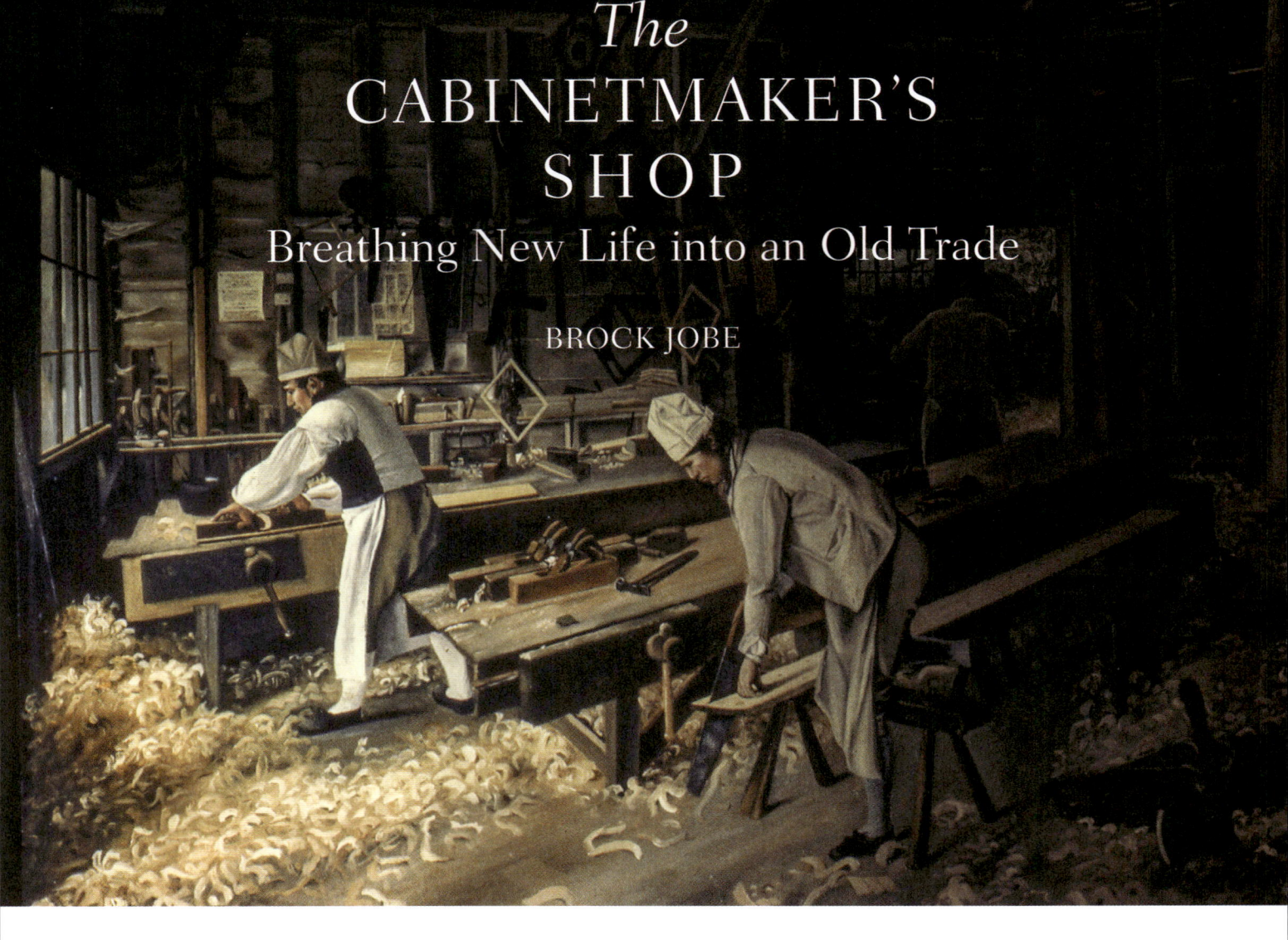

Breathing New Life into an Old Trade

BROCK JOBE

Plans are afoot to build a woodworker's shop at Old Sturbridge Village (OSV). A commitment to craft has long been central to the Sturbridge, Massachusetts museum's mission to recreate a New England community of the early 1800s. Today visitors can see a potter, printer, tinsmith, blacksmith, shoemaker, and cooper in action, and during the early years of the Village, which opened in 1946, cabinet- and chairmakers demonstrated there as well. However, in the mid-1980s, financial pressures and retirements of key craftsmen brought an end to the interpretation of the furniture trades. Now 30 years later, new research on the prominence of cabinetmaking in the Sturbridge area has revived interest in representing the craft to the public.[1]

To design this new shop, village staff will rely on surviving spaces, such as the Luther Sampson shop in Duxbury, Massachusetts, and the photographic and artifactual evidence of the workrooms used by the Dominys of East Hampton, Long Island, and Samuel Wing of Sandwich, Massachusetts.[2] If all goes according to schedule, in June 2021, the Village will mark its 75th anniversary with the opening of the cabinetshop.

As an OSV trustee obsessed with early furniture, I have plunged headfirst into the research and planning for the shop. My focus has narrowed to three topics: the size and appearance of furniture-making shops in America between 1760 and 1830, the outfitting of these shops, and the daily routine of craftsmen. Many scholars have considered these subjects, including Charles Hummel, whose groundbreaking investigation of the Dominy family remains an essential starting point; Scott Landis, whose article "In Search of the Colonial Woodworking Shop" draws several useful comparisons between the Dominy experience and the reconstructed Anthony Hay shop at Colonial Williamsburg; and Mack Headley, who in 1999 explored the cabinetshops of Newport. More recently,

Joshua Klein described the working spaces of Jonathan Fisher, who served the rural village of Blue Hill, Maine, as both minister and woodworker.[3]

I am grateful to everyone who has pondered what it was like to step inside a cabinetshop in the 18th or early 19th century; wondered how large a room it was, how it was lit and heated, how it was furnished, and how a master, often joined by journeymen and apprentices, worked within the space. The search for more detailed answers to these questions has guided the preparation of this article.

As a first step in this process, Bob Roemer, an engineer by profession and Old Sturbridge Village trustee, created a model of the shop. More detailed specifications have followed, fund-raising has commenced, and it is expected that construction will begin in 2020.

Shop Layout

Documentation of the sizes and locations of shops survives in abundance. Simply stated, a woodworking shop could crop up almost anywhere. The rural Maine minister Jonathan Fisher created a workspace in his barn. Two chairmakers in central Massachusetts operated their business in a shop "over the woodshed adjoining the brick house."[4] In 1806, a New Yorker advertised a large stable for rent, noting that "the upper part of said stable was lately used as a cabinet shop, and is well adapted for that purpose."[5] The array of possible shop spaces seems almost endless. An artisan might convert a room in his residence or add an ell along one side, while another workman, especially in an urban area, might choose to rent space in a nearby building. For the most ambitious, a separate structure offered the best solution. The noted Newport cabinetmaker John Goddard attached a large gambrel-roofed shop to the back of his home. His wharf stood nearby, offering Goddard a ready means for shipping his furniture to customers throughout the region. In 1792, the young Boston cabinetmaker, Isaac Vose, kept his shop "within house," but by 1798 he had moved his business into an adjacent two-story shop measuring 27' x 40'. The period account describes the building as "large," suggesting that most work environments were more compact.[6] Indeed, Nathaniel Dominy's workshop, set within an ell of his house, had a footprint of about 15' x 22-1/2', and Samuel Wing's was even smaller.[7]

One of the most informative depictions of a New England shop was drawn by Major John Dunlap, a rural New Hampshire craftsman, working during the late 18th century. His plan "For a Shop" delineated two rooms with a central chimney and doors on three sides (shown on 116). The larger room, measuring 15' x 30', undoubtedly served as the primary workspace. A craftsman needed ample light to work by and easy access for moving furniture in and out. With four windows and two doors, the room filled the bill. The presence of a fireplace offered warmth in the winter as well as a means for heating hide glue. Dunlap's drawing portrays one

John Goddard's gambrel-roofed workshop appears at the back of his home in this 1865 watercolor, *Old Newport Houses*, by Samuel Colman. Courtesy of Whitehorne House Museum Collection, Newport Restoration Foundation, Newport, Rhode Island.

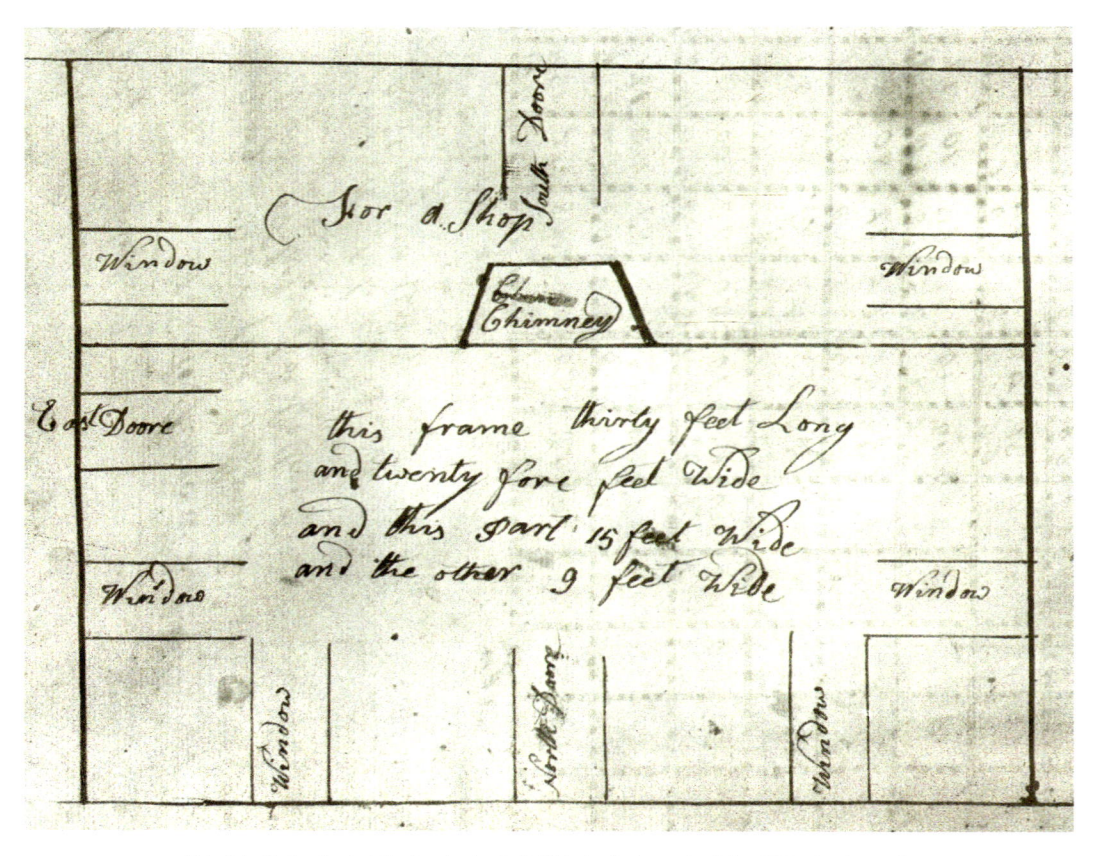

Major John Dunlap sketched this plan of a shop in his Ciphering Book sometime before 1792; privately owned. Courtesy of the New Hampshire Historical Society, Charles S. Parsons Papers, 1987.044.

particular shop plan. Just how typical it was is impossible to say, though it is worth noting that in 1805 Alexander Taylor of Petersburg, Virginia, worked in a shop of the same size.[8] Luther Sampson's shop in Duxbury, Massachusetts, was also of a similar configuration.

Expanding Operations

As the 19th century progressed, more successful craftsmen expanded their operations. Shops increased in size, and many added a "wareroom" for the display of ready-made furniture. Two rare paintings document the larger scale of activity in rural New England. The earlier view records George Bradley's house and shop in Newtown, Connecticut, in 1828 (opposite top). For nearly 30 years, Bradley and his brother Abijah made chairs, three of which can be seen on the second-story porch of his shop.[9] Also, at the rear of the shop appears the unmistakable outline of a woodshed, with its roof pitched in one direction (opposite bottom). These impermanent structures for seasoning and storing timber were commonplace, but rarely survive. Their existence is sometimes noted in insurance surveys, such as that for a cabinetmaker in Lynchburg, Virginia, who in 1805 rented "a cabinet Shop 32 by 20 ½ [feet] with a Shed addition 14 ½ by 20." At Monticello, Thomas Jefferson's design for the "joinery" apparently included a wooden lean-to at one end of the building.[10] While sheds offered a covered space for lumber, the adjoining yard provided room for additional stacks of boards, often laid horizontally with blocks between them to allow air to circulate. At his death in 1797, the Boston cabinetmaker Samuel Fisk kept nearly 4,000 feet of "Bay Mahogony" in a pile outside his shop; "in the Shed" lay two black walnut logs and pieces of maple; an adjacent barn held even more lumber; and within his shop were sawn veneers and boards ready for use. In addition, a mix of materials, described as "Pieces of Mah^y &c [etc.]," were tucked away in the garret above the shop, a location that many craftsmen favored.[11] Certainly that was the case for a Delaware joiner who, on January 6, 1786, recorded that he "puts the Boards I got from McDonald on Shop loft."[12] From all of these accounts, a picture emerges of a crowded scene centered on the shop but spilling out into adjacent areas dotted with timber of every description.

George Bradley's House and Shop, Newtown, Connecticut, 1828. Courtesy of Old Sturbridge Village.

A woodshed with the roof pitched in one direction appears at the back of George Bradley's shop. Courtesy of Old Sturbridge Village.

Two shop signs on the front of the large building in the lower left identify it as a "Furniture Ware Room" and its owner as Mark Elwell. Dudley, Massachusetts, 1831. Courtesy of Old Sturbridge Village.

A second scene, dating from 1831, naively depicts the home and furniture wareroom of Mark Elwell (above). Elwell resided in Dudley, Massachusetts, a mill village near the Connecticut border. He had trained as a traditional cabinetmaker at the end of the 18th century, but by the late 1820s had enlarged his business to compete with neighboring entrepreneurs. One of these, the Southbridge Furniture Ware-House, offered customers "the most extensive assortment of Furniture," including sofas, sideboards, secretaries, drop-leaf tables, stands, bedsteads, and "1000 Chairs, of every description."[13] Like many owners of these establishments, Elwell probably relied on a mix of sources for his stock. Some he and his workmen made; however, the majority came from other suppliers, especially chairmakers throughout the region who assembled tens of thousands of inexpensive Windsor chairs for resale.

In central Massachusetts, a massive cottage industry engaged hundreds of people in the production of chairs. Farmers supplemented their income by sawing planks into roughly shaped chair seats; turners fashioned stretchers, legs, and spindles on water-powered lathes; and chairmakers joined and finished the parts, often commissioning women to make rush seats and decorate the completed objects with paint.[14] The lathe was key to the entire process. While some craftsmen continued to rely on traditional treadle lathes, a sizable number took advantage of the swiftly flowing streams that crisscrossed the area. Their properties became highly prized, as noted in an advertisement of 1827 that included a "valuable stand for a Cabinet or Chairmaker, consisting of a… House and Barn…a two-story Shop with a good Dam on a never-failing stream of water."[15]

Bradley and Elwell's houses stand only a short distance from their shop or wareroom. Might this be artistic license? Probably not, for many accounts confirm that this was often the case. A map of the property of Abiel White, a Weymouth, Massachusetts, cabinetmaker, shows his shop a few steps from his home, and numerous insurance surveys from Virginia document the presence of shops no more than 30 feet from their owners' homes.[16]

By the late 1820s, many ambitious producers had united their operations into individual buildings. The trade card of George Mecke's Northern Cabinet Ware-Rooms in Philadelphia (opposite) perfectly details the vertical integration of his business. Near the entrance, fashionable clients gaze upon an array of elegant mahogany veneered furniture, while above, on the top floor, a journeyman brushes a decorative finish onto a chair. In the foreground, a well-dressed fellow (Mecke or perhaps the shop foreman) and a workman load furniture onto the company's horse-drawn wagon for delivery to a purchaser. Entrepreneurs such as Mecke sought to manage

George Mecke's Northern Cabinet Ware-Rooms, Philadelphia, 1846. Courtesy of The Library Company of Philadelphia.

every aspect of the design, production, and marketing process. Such control had existed a century before in the shops of early America, but the scale had shifted as larger businesses with sizable retail showrooms and greater numbers of specialized workmen became more commonplace. By the 1880s, the most successful operations had grown into factories capable of fabricating more than a million pieces a year.[17]

While cabinetmaking entrepreneurs grew their small shops into multi-level manufactories in the 19th century, the range of tools and outfitting of work spaces changed very little from the previous century. The source of power for a lathe may have switched from the turner's foot or an apprentice's arms (in the case of a great-wheel lathe) to water and later steam, and a few ingenious mechanics had begun to introduce circular saws for slicing veneers during the 1820s.[18] These innovations quickened the pace of processing lumber into usable parts, but traditional methods of construction persisted. Cabinetmakers, chairmakers, and carvers relied on the same tools as their predecessors, and the basic kit identified as early as 1678 by Joseph Moxon remained in place.[19] Saws, planes, chisels, gouges, a brace and bit, awl, marking gauge, hatchet, square, compass, mallet, vise, and bench were as important in the early 19th century as they had been 150 years earlier. Such tools (as well as holdfasts, an iron vise, carving tools, and iron and wooden clamps) were noted in the shop inventory of Samuel Fisk, who died at the young age of 28 in 1797.[20] Fisk had worked as a journeyman for several years before opening an establishment with his younger brother, William, on Washington Street at the southern tip of Boston.[21] Just two workbenches round out the list of equipment in Fisk's shop. The small number suggests that Fisk employed few journeymen or apprentices and may have relied primarily on his brother. The modest operation of the Fisks was not uncommon, even as competing craftsmen set out to expand their output and open warerooms. Some cabinetmakers worked entirely alone, such as William Munroe, who plied the trade from 1799 to 1812 in his shop on the Mill Dam in Concord, Massachusetts.[22]

Sights & Sounds in the Shop

Had you walked into Munroe's establishment or that of Samuel Fisk, what might you have seen? What sights and sounds would have attracted your attention? I have yet to find a detailed period description of the interior of an American cabinetshop. However, the British author George Eliot does peek inside a joiner's establishment in a rural village at the tail end of the 18th century: "The afternoon sun was warm on the five workmen there, busy upon doors and window-frames and wainscoting. A scent of pine-wood from a tentlike pile of planks outside the open door mingled itself with the scent of the elder-bushes which were spreading their summer snow close to the open window opposite; the slanting sunbeams shone through the transparent shavings that flew before the steady plane, and lit up the fine grain of the oak paneling which stood propped against the wall. On a heap of those soft shavings a rough, grey shepherd dog had made himself a pleasant bed, and was lying with his nose between his fore-paws, occasionally wrinkling his brows to cast a glance at the tallest of the five workmen, who was carving a shield in the centre of a wooden mantelpiece."[23]

Though fictional, the account creates an image that calls to mind a joiner's shop portrayed by the English painter George Forster (opposite). Here are multiple benches, an array of tools, and three men at work near windows that filled the space with "slanting sunbeams," as Eliot noted. Later the author describes "the light paper cap" worn by the woodworkers, a useful accessory for keeping dust and shavings out of their hair. Similar caps cover the heads of artisans in Forster's painting, but the practice failed to take hold in America. However, the arrangement of tools does relate to the evidence that survives at the Dominy and Sampson shops (shown on 122). As in the painting, the tools in both shops were mounted in racks or hung from pegs. The configuration might seem haphazard but kept everything within easy reach of craftsmen. Other details in the images depict minor differences. Work-

English joiner's shop, George Forster, 1816. Private collection of Barry and Carol Eisenberg, in memory of Bernard H. Taff; Courtesy of Colonial Williamsburg Foundation.

The Dominy tool collection installed at Winterthur in 1960 in a re-creation of the family's shop in East Hampton, Long Island, remains an unparalleled resource for the study of woodworking practices in early America. Courtesy of Winterthur Museum.

Built about 1789, the Luther Sampson shop in Duxbury, Massachusetts, was rediscovered on the grounds of a private school in 2012. Its intact workbenches, tool racks, and storage cupboard superbly complement the setting presented in the Dominy installation at Winterthur. Courtesy of Jeffrey Klee.

ing in narrower spaces, the American artisans chose to place their benches against the wall and take full advantage of the daylight. In the English shop, the joists above offered storage space while the open framing at the gable end (shown on 121) allowed long boards to stand upright ready for use. The American counterparts had second-floor lofts, which limited the storage of timbers vertically.

In none of the three shops does a fireplace or stove appear, but that visual absence may be misleading. In the Sampson shop, evidence of an original chimney stack survives, and in Forster's painting only a portion of the workroom is shown, leaving open the possibility that the unseen area contained a stove. After 1790, most American shops, especially those in free-standing structures, had a fireplace or stove (shown on 124). And with that always came the danger of fire, as chronicled on one sad occasion in 1798: "Some small children…in attempting to kindle a fire in the stove with pine shavings, let them drop on the floor…and immediately set the surrounding shavings in a flame, and soon left the room, and shut the door. The workmen being absent, it was impossible to extinguish the fire."[24] The Wrentham, Massachusetts, cabinetmaker Silas Metcalf lost his entire cabinetshop, along with his tools, timber, and unfinished furniture. Though a devastating loss, Metcalfe managed to save his house and barn "by the united exertions of a number of the adjoining neighbours."[25]

The Craftsmen

How I wish we could have viewed Metcalfe's shop before the fire or walked into the workrooms of Luther Sampson and the Dominy family when they had active businesses. Just a few minutes with Silas Metcalfe would tell us so much more than we can glean from a bill or receipt. Hundreds of account books, daybooks, ledgers, and the like document the activities of furniture craftsmen. Yet, the personal side of these individuals – their character, beliefs, abilities, work ethic, and daily routines – is so very difficult to discern. Journals, diaries, and autobiographies offer a start. To date, I have located four of these for American furniture craftsmen. The earliest, and briefest, was kept by an artisan near Wilmington, Delaware, from May 19, 1785, until January 11, 1786. He never recorded his name in the document but subsequent research has suggested that it may be William Johnston, a carpenter and joiner of Mill Creek Hundred.[26] The next is a lengthy handwritten autobiography by William Munroe of Concord, Massachusetts. In 1839, at the age of 61, Munroe recounted his life in engaging detail. While his narrative offers observations on many topics, it is his experiences as a young man, when he trained to be a cabinetmaker and worked at his trade for about a dozen years, that are most relevant here.[27] A third author, Samuel Seabury, also looked back upon his early years in the furniture trade, describing the travails of his aborted apprenticeship in New York City in 1815 and 1816.[28] The final writer, Enos White, began a diary at the age of 18 in Weymouth, Massachusetts, in 1821, and for the next 30 years continually commented on his challenges as a woodworker and farmer within a changing economic climate.[29]

Apprenticeship figured prominently in Munroe and Seabury's accounts. The process was difficult and fraught with obstacles. For Seabury, apprenticeship proved to be a mistake, which he was able to undo in less than a year. The son of a minister, he had more education than most boys and ultimately did follow in the footsteps of his father and grandfather. Initially a different path was projected for young Samuel. His father wanted "to bring up his children as mechanics in which capacity he thought they would have the least temptation to forfeit the virtues of sobriety and honesty and stand the best chance to reap the advantages of frugal and industrious habits." A worthy goal perhaps, but one Samuel found ill-suited to his abilities. "The truth is," reminisced Seabury many years later, "I had a most astonishing inaptitude for all mechanical employments." Yet, given his father's insistence, apprenticeship in a trade had become a foregone conclusion, the only question was which one. In October 1815, the elder Seabury traveled from his home on Long Island to New York, where he learned that the cabinetmaker William Mandeville had immediate need of an additional apprentice. A deal was struck that would place Samuel in the shop on a temporary basis, with the understanding that an apprenticeship could follow if his work was satisfactory. The following month father and son set off to the city to meet the lad's new master. In his recollections, penned as a series of 11 letters, Samuel adopted Dickensian names for everyone he encountered. Mandeville became "Mr. Moneygripe."[30] At noon, "my father parted from me and I proceeded with my trunk to Mr. Moneygripe's." A richly detailed description of his master's establishment followed: "His residence was a two story house with [a] brick front in the heart of the city. The front of the building both above and below was used as a warehouse. In the rear was a small addition which was used as a dwelling house and again in the rear of this was a large two story building which constituted the workshop. Under the workshop was a cellar which answered the double purpose of a kitchen and an eating room. Every part of the yard except

Stoves were a frequent fixture of shops in the early 19th century and with them came the ever-present possibility of a devastating fire. Edward Hazen, *The Panorama of Professions and Trades* (Philadelphia, 1836), 219. Courtesy of Winterthur Library.

a small alley that went round the building was piled with lumber; and a large frame in the extreme rear and a cellar under the warehouse were two other depositories for the same material."[31]

Like Duncan Phyfe and other prominent New York cabinetmakers, Mandeville managed both warerooms for the display and sale of furniture and a production shop. Samuel quickly learned that his responsibilities lay in both places. As the newest apprentice, he was given the most mundane tasks: dusting furniture in the warerooms, heating a glue pot in the shop, carrying mahogany joists to a nearby turner to be transformed into bed posts, or helping to load a sideboard onto a wheelbarrow and carting it to a customer's home. Mr. Moneygripe kept tight control over the apprentices, often bellowing a wake-up call in the morning and instructions during the day. Training in the trade came slowly. Typically an apprentice had to run errands for a year before gaining access to tools. Samuel did receive permission to use a saw and jack plane sooner, but "fresh occurrences were happening every day to disgust me with my situation."[32]

Throughout his letters, Samuel never discussed the interiors of the warerooms or shop. Instead it was his fellow apprentices that attracted his attention. An entertaining account of the group ranks among Seabury's most noteworthy passages. He first met John, "a dirty vulgar looking fellow," who considered the new arrival as "an important acquisition on whom he was henceforward to turn off the most disagreeable part of his labors." John then spent a few minutes characterizing his fellow apprentices during a visit to the shop:

The oldest was John Sobersides – the son of a respectable farmer at Jamaica – very steady – best apprentice Baas had ever had – would be out of his time in about six months. The next was Ike Redface – a rale clever fellow – a better hand at work than the other, but he liked a horn of brandy and would lie as fast as a horse could trot. The next was Bill SaintJohn – hadn't been here long – thought himself a pretty smart chap – was always reading when he got a chance and could talk dic (dictionary words) equal to any fellow. The fourth was Alf Hothead – a good natured fellow – if you'd let him have his way – but a most a hell of a temper [sic] – throw a jack-plane at your head as quick as [a] wink...[33]

John's colorful comments, as recounted by Seabury, afforded a rare glimpse of the various personalities that worked within a larger cabinetshop. It was a disparate crew, bound only by their common connection to Mr. Moneygripe. Journeymen were also present in the shop, but Seabury never mentions them by name. They held a more elevated status and operated independently of the apprentices. No doubt the two groups interacted, yet one would never know it from Seabury's memories of his time in the shop.

By late spring of 1816, Seabury had reached a breaking point. Moneygripe ordered him to make a packing crate for some furniture that was about to be shipped. He received the dimensions and made the crate, only to discover that the dimensions were of the furniture, not the crate. His crate was too small, and with that: "I flung the hammer upon the ground, went up stairs and packed my trunk and in the course of half an hour took an eternal adieu of Moneygripe and all his concerns."[34] Seabury's unusual status as a fledgling workman not yet bound as an apprentice allowed him the liberty of walking away. He pursued a field much more to his liking, gaining an academic degree at Columbia and achieving success as a teacher and cleric. Though only a member of the cabinetmaking community for seven months, Seabury made an invaluable contribution – his portrayal of craft life explores the lowest level of the shop experience, a tale rarely told in period documents.

Unlike Samuel Seabury, William Munroe did complete his apprenticeship and for more than a decade profited handsomely from his trade. However, he faced many obstacles throughout his training. His story illustrates the vicissitudes of adolescence, as a confident teenager makes his way in the world. After laboring through several years of trying different trades and finding them not to his liking, William discovered that he had an aptitude for the work of a cabinetmaker. Several short-lived arrangements with nearby shops led him to turn to a distant relation, Nehemiah Munroe, who operated a successful business in Roxbury, Massachusetts. Nehemiah Munroe took an active interest in training apprentices and accorded William greater responsibility over time. He had finally found a satisfactory situation and stayed until December 1799, when he reached the age of 21. "During my apprenticeship," he observed with honesty and a bit of pride, "I had become the best workman in the shop. All extra work that required nicety, carved work or any new fashion that had not been made in the shop before was committed to me."[35] After working briefly as a journeyman, William moved to Concord, where he shared a building with his brother Daniel, a prominent clockmaker. Both brothers benefited from the relationship. Daniel now had a supplier of clock cases and William could rely on a steady income, which he supplemented through the sale of other furniture forms. For a decade William continued in his trade, but by 1812, he found it increasingly difficult to work as a traditional cabinetmaker in what was essentially a one-man shop. He lamented "that I could not dispose of so much furniture as I could make with my own hands, Business of every kind extremely bad; Clocks fast going out of fashion, My family expences at the same time increasing."[36] In his search for another source of income, he discovered pencil making, and, as they say, the rest is history. His annual income rose from $700 to $7,000.[37] His autobiography is a story of success, but it is the ups and downs of his five apprenticeships that most captured my interest. How typical was his experience? It is impossible to say with certainty. Yet I suspect, if we had comparable accounts for other apprentices, we would find that the path to practicing as a professional tradesman was far rockier and more circuitous than we might suppose.

The final two narratives barely touch upon apprenticeship and instead chronicle the adult careers of their authors. The first covers only eight months of an unnamed rural joiner's activities in Delaware during the 1780s. Yet from that snippet emerges a detailed picture of a well-established craftsman with extensive connections throughout the region. He employed three workmen, including an apprentice named John Eleck, and sometimes assembled crews of local hands to assist in larger projects. Like many country artisans, his day varied considerably and changed with the seasons. In May and June we find him at work in his shop building a tea table, dining table, chest, desk, and coffin, making a jack plane for his own use, purchasing wood from nearby farmers, planting potatoes for himself and others, meeting on business with numerous neighbors, and traveling to Wilmington and Philadelphia. In July he devoted much of his time to cutting hay. In October he began to build a carriage house (described as a "chair house") for one friend and raised the frame of a residence for another. Over the course of the entire diary, several issues become apparent that many craftsmen faced. The most obvious was the likelihood of injury or illness. "This day I am much indisposed I believe from working out in the sun [the day before]," the joiner wrote on a hot July day. Falls, cuts, and various wounds limited his work on numerous occasions, with one particular incident proving especially serious. "This morning," he wrote on October 12, "I go to Thos Wallaces and Joins his frame [joins the frame of his house] but not six Minutes until by lifting a piece of Scantling I strain'd my back that makes me unable to work." Days later he could still not stand or sit, and almost two weeks passed before he could return to a full schedule.[38] The reality of disease or injury affected everyone but for a tradesman any setback could be devastating.

Another complicating factor in the joiner's daily routine was that it was remarkably varied and at times seemed to change with little forethought – a friend shows up at his house, and off they go hunting or fishing. On June 18, "this Morning I begin to work at Table [his term for workbench] but Cap.t McKennon soon comes and Causes me Qu[i]t work and prepare for going a fishing we start about 11 oclock & comes home by dark with middling success."[39] With the exception of house framing projects

In Mr. Moneygripe's cabinetshop journeymen carried out the majority of work, while apprentices were left to perform the most mundane tasks, from dusting furniture in the warerooms to making cases in which to ship finished goods. Edward Hazen, *The Panorama of Professions and Trades* (Philadelphia, 1836), 221. Courtesy of Winterthur Library.

that might have required several days of continual labor, the joiner's schedule differed from day to day. His time making furniture rarely filled an entire day. He never seemed to be in a hurry to finish a particular piece (barring coffins) and frequently relied on his apprentice or journeyman to assist him. An urban cabinetmaker, especially in a larger city such as Philadelphia or Boston, undoubtedly spent far more of his day on furniture. However, among larger shops, it was the journeymen who stayed busy at their work, typically working until 6 p.m., while the master managed the business, sought new customers, and set design standards for the furniture.[40]

The author of the final narrative, Enos White, maintained a diary from 1821 until 1850. His opening remarks express the ambition of a young adult anxious to face the world, writing on November 21, 1821, "This Day I leave my Fathers after haveing got him to consent to my being Free I leave in Good Spirits although my prospects are very small, and the Opinion of my Friends is that I shall soon wish myself back again I am now Eighteen Years and five months Old with one Decent Suit of Cloths and fifteen Dollars in Cash to Comence my Carreer with." Over the next two years he worked for several people, including his brother, Lemuel, who operated a cabinetshop in their hometown of Weymouth, about 15 miles south of Boston. Every job left him despondent. "I am Sick of my Business," Enos announced on May 10, 1823, "am resolved to work Cabinet Making at home or go to Sea." A trip to the Boston docks immediately turned him against the life of a sailor. Only one option remained. Borrowing $75 from his grandmother, he opened a cabinetshop in Weymouth, much to his brother's displeasure. Business was brisk. After six months, he reported that "I still continue to work for myself and find the more I Doe the mor I find to Doe."[41] For Lemuel, his brother represented increased competition. To reduce the threat, the two entered into a partnership, but this was destined for failure and within six months Lemuel had left town in search of other work. Enos was once again on his own. He hired two boys to work with him, and after their short stint, he took on an apprentice. Over the next two years White prospered in this trade, thanks to a steady demand for his furniture combined with his own commitment to hard work and a thrifty lifestyle. His efforts enabled him to buy his father's shop, his brother's tools and lumber, and half of a dwelling house.

White celebrated with pride what he had accomplished "by the sweat of the Brow without the assistance of anyone." But several years later, furniture sales declined, and White found himself in a similar predicament to that of William Munroe two decades earlier. A new business plan was needed. In 1830, White ventured into an ill-fated partnership to open a shoe store in Cincinnati, Ohio. After much time and effort to secure a location and procure inventory, White and his partner were unable to turn a profit. As options dissolved for the business, White contracted typhus fever and spent weeks bedridden. After he had recovered sufficiently to travel, he returned home. As disatrous as his Ohio experiment had been, he had no misgivings. "Although I know it has been a Dear lessen to me but still I dont regret it for I have learnt more of the world than I should if I had staid at home all my Life."[42]

Back in Weymouth, Enos White returned to furniture making, assisted off and on by three hired hands. Then came an offer from his brother Lemuel, now engaged in the surgical instrument business. Wooden boxes for these instruments were needed and Enos agreed to supply them. In April and May of 1835, he made 1,650 boxes, and another 1,000 in the following year. White remained in Weymouth for the remainder of his life. During the late 1830s he took over his father's farm, tried his hand at shoe making, and scaled back his furniture-making business, focusing primarily on looking-glass frames once the market for specialized boxes declined.

The diary of Enos White depicts a determined and independent risk-taker, who continually sought new schemes for earning a living and caring for his family. White prided himself on his own abilities and work ethic. Compare his actions to that of the Delaware joiner, who appeared to lack the same level of persistence and commitment, but had deeper connections within his community. Samuel Seabury was never cut out to be a woodworker, but left us an enlightening exposé of the lowest rung of the craft ladder. William Munroe achieved a solid reputation in the cabinet trade but could not sustain his small solitary business amid the advent and swelling popularity of furniture warerooms. The stories embedded in these four accounts enhance our understanding of what it meant to be a cabinetmaker in America during the late 18th and early 19th centuries. Taken together, these narratives, along with the evidence gleaned from surviving cabinetshops, historic tool collections, and public records, breathe life into the past.

As Old Sturbridge Village moves forward with plans to build a shop and interpret the cabinetmaking experience, we seek to tap all of these sources, so that you will not only see traditional woodworking in an appropriate space but learn about the lives of the makers and their customers. Perhaps you will meet old Mr. Moneygripe or a young Enos White, intent on earning a living in a changing world. Come take a look in 2021. ◆

ENDNOTES

1. Although Old Sturbridge Village has lacked a permanent cabinetmaking presence since the mid-1980s, the institution has mounted occasional exhibitions on the subject, the most notable being a display of central Massachusetts furniture in 1993 and 1994. At that time, Donna K. Baron, Frank G. White, and Karen L. Blanchfield carried out extensive research on Worcester County cabinetmaking, which resulted in four unpublished research reports and three articles: Frank G. White, "Wing and Reed, Case Studies of Two Early Nineteenth-Century Chairmakers," *Eighteenth-Century Woodworking Tools, Papers Presented at a Tool Symposium, May 19-22, 1994, Colonial Williamsburg Historic Trades, Volume III*, edited by James M. Gaynor (Williamsburg, VA: Colonial Williamsburg, 1997), 199-214; Donna Keith Baron: "Furniture Makers and Retailers in Worcester County, Massachusetts, Working to 1850," *The Magazine Antiques* 143:5 (May 1993), 784-795, and Donna K. Baron, "Definition and Diaspora of Regional Style: The Worcester County Model," *American Furniture 1995*, edited by Luke Beckerdite and William N. Hosley (Milwaukee: Chipstone Foundation, 1995), 167-190.
2. See Christopher Schwarz, "A Visit to the Sampson Joinery Shop in Duxbury, Mass.," blog post, May 18, 2013; online: https://blog.lostartpress.com/2013/05/18/a-visit-to-the-sampson-joinery-shop-in-duxbury-mass/; Tom Whalen, "In Search of 'L•SAMPSON'," *The Chronicle of the Early American Industries Association* 69:3 (Sept. 2016), 6-9; Peter Follansbee, "Everybody Who Knows 'Why' Is Dead," *Mortise & Tenon* Issue Two (2016), 50-51; Charles F. Hummel, *With Hammer in Hand, The Dominy Craftsmen of East Hampton, New York* (Charlottesville, VA: The University Press of Virginia, 1968), 6-11; Shelley Cathcart and Amy Griffin, "On the Trail of Two Cabinetmakers, Reconstructing the Careers of Samuel Wing & Tilly Mead," *Mortise & Tenon* Issue Three (2017), 106-111.
3. Hummel, *With Hammer in Hand*; Scott Landis, "In Search of the Colonial Woodworking Shop: Benches, Shops, and the Woodworking Process," *Eighteenth-Century Woodworking Tools, Papers Presented at a Tool Symposium, May 19-22, 1994*, 163-180; Mack Headley, "Eighteenth-Century Cabinet Shops and the Furniture-Making Trades in Newport, Rhode Island," *American Furniture 1999*, edited by Luke Beckerdite (Milwaukee: Chipstone Foundation, 1999), 17-47; Joshua A. Klein, *Hands Employed Aright: The Furniture Making of Jonathan Fisher (1768-1847)* (Fort Mitchell, KY: Lost Art Press, 2018), 33-67; Follansbee, "Everybody Who Knows 'Why' Is Dead," 50-51; Cathcart and Griffin, "On the Trail of Two Cabinetmakers," 106-111.
4. Insurance policy for Silas Lamson, Worcester Mutual Fire Insurance Company, Dec. 12, 1837, Conant Papers, Worcester Historical Museum.
5. *The People's Friend & Daily Advertiser* (New York), Dec. 1, 1806.
6. Patricia E. Kane, *Art & Industry in Early America: Rhode Island Furniture, 1650-1830* (New Haven: Yale University Art Gallery, 2016), 50-51; Robert D. Mussey Jr., and Clark Pearce, *Rather Elegant Than Showy: The Classical Furniture of Isaac Vose* (Boston: Massachusetts Historical Society, 2018), 33, 35; Direct Tax List of 1798 for Massachusetts and Maine, 1798. R. Stanton Avery Special Collections, New England Historic Genealogical Society, Boston, MA, vol. 7, 349; online: https://www.americanancestors.org/databases/massachusetts-and-maine-direct-tax-1798/image?volumeId=13123&pageName=349&rId=234299333.
7. The Historic American Buildings Survey documented the original dimensions of the Dominy woodworking shop when the Dominy residence was studied in 1940; see Hummel, *With Hammer in Hand*, 6-11; Cathcart and Griffin, 107.
8. The figure shown on 116 omits written instructions on one side of the page for making a cradle; for an illustration of the entire document, see *The Dunlaps & Their Furniture* (Manchester, NH: The Currier Gallery of Art, 1970), 65; insurance policy for Alexander Taylor, May 26, 1798, Mutual Assurance Society of Virginia, vol. 10, 116. Thanks to June Lucas, Museum of Early Southern Decorative Arts, for directing me to Southern newspaper ads and insurance policies available through the MESDA Craftsman Database, a magnificent resource for anyone interested in the history of craft in early America.
9. The cabinetmaker Benjamin A. Winston occupied a shop owned by Samuel Irvine; see insurance policy for Samuel Irvine, Nov. 20, 1805, Mutual Assurance Society of Virginia, vol. 62, 401, MESDA Craftsman Database.
10. I am indebted to Gardiner Hallock, Robert H. Smith Director of Restoration, Curatorial, and Historic Facilities at Monticello, for this information; Hallock to Brock Jobe, email correspondence, November 26, 2018.
11. Estate inventory of Samuel Fisk, Boston, recorded Jan. 30, 1797, Suffolk County Probate File Papers, Boston, MA; online: https://www.americanancestors.org/databases/suffolk-county-ma-probate-file-papers/image?pageName=20668:6&volumeId=48702&rId=69626020.
12. Diary of unidentified joiner, possibly William Johnston, Mill Creek Hundred, DE, Jan. 6, 1786, Winterthur Library.
13. *Southbridge Register*, Feb. 17, 1829. For an image of this ad, see Donna K. Baron and Karen L. Blanchfield, "Selling Worcester County Furniture 1820-1850: New Methods and New Markets" (unpublished research report, Old Sturbridge Village, Feb. 10, 1993).
14. Frank G. White, "Chair Making in Northern Worcester County" (unpublished research report, Old Sturbridge Village, Feb. 10, 1993), 2-10.
15. The property was located in the town of Royalston in central Massachusetts, just south of the New Hampshire border; *Massachusetts Spy* (Worcester), March 28, 1827.
16. Derin Tyler Bray, "Urban Craft in Rural Massachusetts: The Weymouth Cabinetmaking Shop of Abiel White, 1790-1851" (master's thesis, University of Delaware, 2006), fig. 2.7; for Southern examples, see insurance policy for Alexander Taylor cited in note 8.
17. The Massachusetts chair factories of the Heywood Brothers in Gardner and Cyrus Wakefield in what is now Wakefield ranked among the largest of these late 19th-century operations. They merged in 1897; see *A Completed Century, 1826-1926: The Story of Heywood-Wakefield Company* (Boston, 1926), 1-27.
18. Robert D. Mussey Jr., "Adam Stewart, engineer/inventor, designer/builder of Baldwin Mills, Boston, Massachusetts, 1825" (unpublished paper, March 31, 2014). I am deeply grateful to Robert Mussey for his assistance throughout the preparation of this article.
19. Joseph Moxon, *Mechanick Exercises, or the Doctrine of Handy-Works* (1703; repr., New York: Praeger Publishers, 1970), "Joyner's Work," pl. 4. For Moxon's discussion of joinery, see 63-116.
20. Estate inventory of Samuel Fisk, Boston, recorded Jan. 30, 1797, Suffolk County Probate File Papers, Boston, MA; online: https://www.americanancestors.org/databases/suffolk-county-ma-probate-file-papers/image?pageName=20668:6&volumeId=48702&rId=69626020.
21. On June 4, 1792 Samuel and William Fisk purchased land on Washington Street, Boston, and over the next five years took out a series of mortgages. See Boston, MA: Inhabitants and Estates of the Town of Boston, 1630-1822 (Thwing Collection), New England Historic Genealogical Society, online: https://www.americanancestors.org/databases/boston-ma-inhabitants-and-estates-of-the-town-of-boston-1630-1822-thwing-collection/image?volumeId=14226&pageName=8097&rId=260104941.
22. David F. Wood, "'The Best Workman in the Shop': Cabinetmaker William Munroe of Concord," in *Boston Furniture, 1700-1900*, edited by Brock Jobe and Gerald W. R. Ward (Boston: Colonial Society of Massachusetts, 2016), 220.
23. George Eliot (Mary Ann Evans), *Adam Bede* (1859; electronic repr., Project Gutenberg, 2006: https://www.gutenberg.org/files/507/507-h/507-h.htm#link2HCH0001), chap. 1, "The Workshop."
24. *Federal Gazette* (Boston), Jan. 30, 1798.
25. Ibid.
26. Diary of unidentified joiner, 1785-1786, Winterthur Library. The library's finding aid for the diary states that "external evidence suggests that William Johnston was the keeper of the volume. He was a cabinetmaker and joiner in Mill Creek Hundred, New Castle County, Delaware." However, the diary's author refers on many occasions to "Billy Johnson" and in one case borrows planes from him. Might the lender of the planes be William Johnston? If so, the writer of the diary remains a mystery. In 1988, Barbara McLean Ward used the diary as the basis for her article, "The Joiner of Mill Creek Hundred," in *After Ratification, Material Life in Delaware, 1789-1820*, edited by J. Ritchie Garrison, *et al* (Newark, DE: University of Delaware, 1988), 79-97. Ward refuted the attribution of the diary to William Johnston.
27. David Wood brilliantly analyzed Munroe's autobiography in the article cited in note 22.
28. Robert Bruce Mullin, ed., *Moneygripe's Apprentice, The Personal Narrative of Samuel Seabury III* (New Haven: Yale University Press, 1989).
29. Diary of Enos White, 1821-1851, Winterthur Library. Enos was the son of Abiel White, a Weymouth cabinetmaker, whose career was analyzed by Derin Bray in the master's thesis cited in note 16.
30. Quotations from Mullin, *Moneygripe's Apprentice*, 46, 80. The editor connects Moneygripe to Mandeville in 60, fn. 5. For information on Mandeville, see Peter M. Kenny, "A Recent Gift Sheds New Light on Duncan Phyfe and the New York School of Cabinetmaking," *Classica Americana* blog post, Classical American Homes Preservation Trust; online: https://classicalamericanhomes.org/essay/a-recent-gift-sheds-new-light-on-duncan-phyfe-and-the-new-york-school-of-cabinetmaking/.
31. Mullin, *Moneygripe's Apprentice*, 60-61.
32. Ibid., 79.
33. Ibid., 61-63.
34. Ibid., 81.
35. Quoted in Wood, "'The Best Workman in the Shop,'" 210.
36. Quoted in ibid., 213, 220.
37. Ibid., 221.
38. The three workmen were John McCormick, Jimmy Montgomery, and an apprentice named John Eleck. The quoted passages in the diary of the unidentified joiner appear under the dates of July 10 and Oct. 12, 1785.
39. Quoted in ibid., June 18, 1785.
40. The routine workday of 6 a.m. to 6 p.m. for cabinetmakers is recorded in Robert Campbell, *The London Tradesman* (1747; repr., Devon, England: David & Charles, 1969), 332. In George Eliot's *Adam Bede*, which describes a joiner's shop in 1799, quitting time is also cited as 6 p.m.; see note 23, chap. 1, "The Workshop." The role of the master in a large late 18th-century London shop is described by Justus Moser, a German visitor; see Christopher Gilbert, *Life and Works of Thomas Chippendale* (London: Cassell, 1978), 22.
41. Diary of Enos White, 1, 3.
42. Ibid., 7, 39, 40.

FORGING TRADITIONS
The Common Ancestry of Japanese & Western Edge Tools

WILBUR PAN

Japanese tools are often discussed in terms of how they are different than Western tools. That's what I heard when I first got into woodworking and considered picking up some Japanese tools. In the time that I've been using them, I've come to a different conclusion: There are more similarities than differences between the two, if one knows where to look.

When I first started getting into woodworking, there seemed to be two camps – power-tool users and hand-tool users. And among the hand-tool users, there was this world of Japanese tools. I'm of Chinese descent, and probably because of the Asian connection, I gravitated toward these tools, which were described as having incredible properties. Compared to Western tools, they were said to be able to be sharpened to a finer edge, and to hold that edge for longer. Who wouldn't want to use these tools?

There was one problem. I completely believed that Japanese tools could have these properties, but I couldn't find good information on why Japanese tools had the properties that they did. At that time, there were three main sources of information regarding Japanese tools that I could find. The first was Toshio Odate's book, *Japanese Woodworking Tools: Their Tradition, Spirit, and Use*, which to this day is the bible of Japanese tool information as far as I am concerned. But although Odate had elegant descriptions of Japanese tools, how they could be sharpened to a fine degree, and how their edges lasted so long, he doesn't give an explanation as to why.

The other two sources were less useful. Information could be gotten from sellers of Japanese tools, who often told a story about how the blacksmith came from a generations-long line of blacksmiths, how he dedicated his life to making Japanese plane blades or chisels, but that now he was old and his children would not carry on the family tradition – so I should buy the plane or chisel before he died. These were lovely stories, but didn't help me as to why the tools worked the way they did.

The other source of information was the internet. Unfortunately, many of the people on the internet seemed to be less than forthcoming about what they knew about Japanese tools. Alternatively, there were people who would talk about the Zen of using these tools, and how one needed to deeply understand the philosophy of the East to truly appreciate the nuances of these tools. I thought this was a curious point of view, as no one seemed to invoke Aristotle or Thomas Aquinas when discussing Western hand tools.

I think this is where my background and upbringing helped guide me to a better understanding of Japanese tools. My father is a physics professor, and for as long as I can remember, he taught me that everything in the natural world could be explained by scientific principles. Also, having been raised in a Chinese family, I wasn't overly impressed by Zen and the Eastern mysticism that people seemed to want to attach to Japanese tools.[1]

Japanese Blade Construction

In trying to understand Japanese tools, I settled on a few postulates. First, despite the fact that Japanese (and Asian) woodworking traditions seemed to develop without any input from the Western world, it seemed that Japanese woodworkers had the same goals as Western woodworkers. They had sharp pieces of metal that they used to shape wood to build things as efficiently as possible.

Second, although the species of wood used in Asian and Western woodworking may be different, at some level physics takes over, and the interaction of the tools and these species of wood had to be pretty much the same. And so, although Japanese tools might look like they are quite different than Western tools, with the laminated construction of plane blades and chisels, and the hollows on the backs, I thought there were more similarities than differences between the two, if one would only look for them.

As a starting point in understanding Japanese tools, it's probably best to examine how they are made. And even before looking at how they are made, it's good to look at steel, and how steel works. In its simplest form, steel is a combination of iron and carbon. Pure iron consists of atoms of iron that arrange themselves naturally into a cubic structure. This cubic structure is not rigid, however. The cubic structure can move, which is why pure iron is

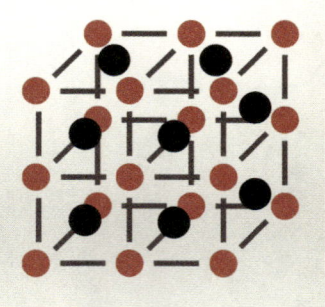

Iron

Iron + Carbon = Steel

malleable, and can be hammered and shaped into forms that are useful for us.

Carbon happens to be just the right size so that if it is able to get into the gaps of the cubic structure of iron, it can stiffen the structure so that its ability to move is greatly restrained. The addition of just 0.5-2 percent of carbon to iron can cause this to happen, creating carbides that are small and hard. These carbides are suspended in a matrix that ultimately makes steel. This is why steel is much harder than pure iron. This hardness is what allows steel to take an edge, and have that edge hold up to abrasive forces, such as being pushed through a piece of wood.

In terms of history, this was first developed in China around 500 B.C., and spread throughout the rest of Asia from there. The oldest examples of ironware in Japan appear around 300 B.C. In Japan, the raw materials to make steel came from iron-rich sand deposits, and charcoal, which supplied both a heat source and carbon.

The Japanese method of making steel starts with a clay furnace called a *tatara*. After constructing the tatara, iron-rich sand and charcoal are loaded into it. The charcoal is set on fire, and the fire is tended for three days. At the end of that process, chunks of steel, looking like miniature meteorites, can be retrieved from the tatara. These pieces of steel vary in their properties. Some are softer, and can be used like wrought iron or cast iron. But some of the steel pieces are very hard, and can be used for tool steel, or for swordmaking. This process of making steel was fairly well standardized by the 8th-9th century in Japan.

Creating a hard piece of steel is not without its challenges. Any given piece of steel has a balance of hardness and toughness, which is the ability to resist cracking under impact. Harder steel is more abrasion-resistant, so if it is used to make an edge tool, the edge can last longer. But hard steels are also brittle, and can crack under impact. Tougher steels are less hard, so they won't crack, but they also won't hold an edge for long.

If a blacksmith forge-welds a piece of soft steel and hard steel together, the two layers work together to overcome their weaknesses. The hard layer of steel can be used as the cutting edge, while the soft layer of steel can provide strength to the tool, preventing it from cracking.

Japanese plane blades and chisels combine the best properties of both steels through this laminated construction. The cutting edge and back of these tools are made of hard steel, while the top part is mainly made of the soft steel. Japanese swords were made in a similar manner, with two pieces of softer steel forge-welded onto a harder piece of steel in the middle. This technology was perfected many centuries ago. There are flawless examples of Japanese swords and daggers with this laminated construction that date back to the 1300s.

Sharpening Japanese tools is easy. Their laminated structure means that the hard steel layer can be quite thin. Working the bevel requires that the sharpening medium has to wear away only 1/8" or less of hard steel. The soft layer is so soft that it isn't a factor in the sharpening process. The backside of the tool, however, is entirely of hard steel, and so would be a bear to flatten were it a flat layer. That is why the blacksmith makes a hollow on the backside of chisels and plane blades. This is most commonly done by hammering a hollow into the backside during the forging process, then refining the hollow with scrapers. Because only a small area near the cutting edge and the perimeter of the back needs to be flattened, this task is much easier than were the entire back of the tool flat.

The forge-welding process offers some other advantages to tools made using this process. Any piece of steel relies on carbides that form during the heat-treating process for hardness and edge retention. Typical modern Western chisels and plane blades usually are made of O1 or A2 steel. These steels have carbides that are in the 10-13 micron range.

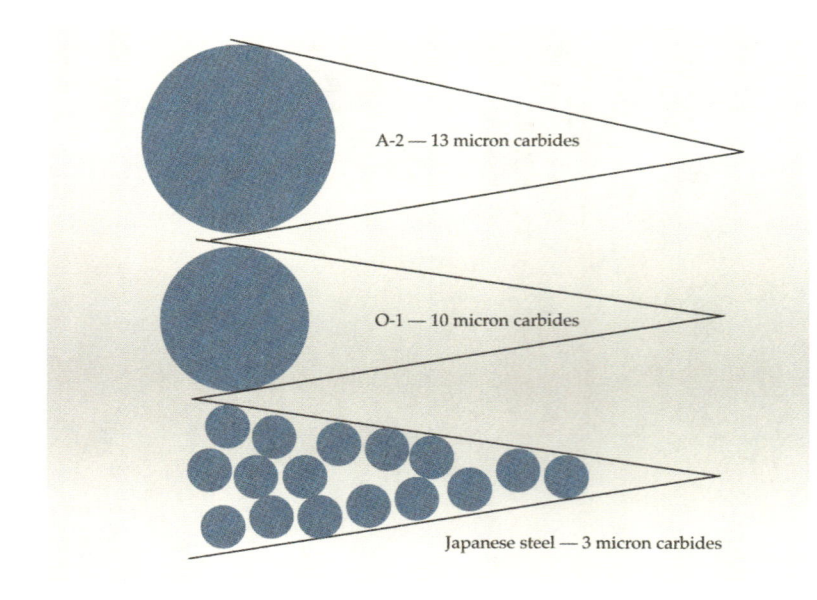

In comparison, we know that traditionally made forge-welded tools can have carbides as small as 3 microns from examining Damascus swords, which are made using the same process of forge-welding softer layers of steel to a hard piece of steel that forms the cutting edge. This is partly due to the repeated impact of the blacksmith's hammer on the tool during the forge-welding process, which helps to break down the carbides and distribute them more evenly throughout the hard steel layer.

These smaller carbides allow for more support at the cutting edge of the tool, which leads to better edge retention. Sharpening is also easier, because it's easier to remove a thin layer of smaller carbides to restore the edge than the larger carbides seen in O1 or A2 steel.

Most modern Western chisels have obvious differences from forge-welded laminated tools, the main one being that they are made of a single piece of steel. As noted above, this piece of steel can't be too hard, because it would be too brittle to withstand impact and be prone to cracking. Because of this, modern Western chisels are hardened to a lesser degree than Japanese chisels, so they don't have the same degree of edge retention.[2]

A Common Ancestry

It wasn't always this way, however. Back in the day, Western blacksmiths also forge-welded harder pieces of steel to softer pieces of steel to make plane blades and chisels, as can clearly be seen by examining older Western plane blades and chisels. Earlier 20th-century examples of Stanley plane blades also have this laminated construction.

Western blacksmiths also would hammer or grind slight hollows into the backside of plane blades and chisels to make flattening the back easier, although this wasn't taken to the same degree of refinement as in Japanese tools (shown opposite). In speaking with many modern blacksmiths who make tools, this technique is still used. Some Western toolmakers including Ashley Iles examine their tools during the manufacturing process to make sure that the concave side is on the back, even though these tools are not laminated.

So what happened in the Western toolmaking world that resulted in the switch from laminated construction to using a single piece of steel? The most obvious factor is the Industrial Revolution. If you are going to mass-produce a chisel in a factory environment in the late 1800s, it's going to be very difficult to reproduce the forge-welding process. The ability to forge-weld a hard piece of steel to a softer piece of

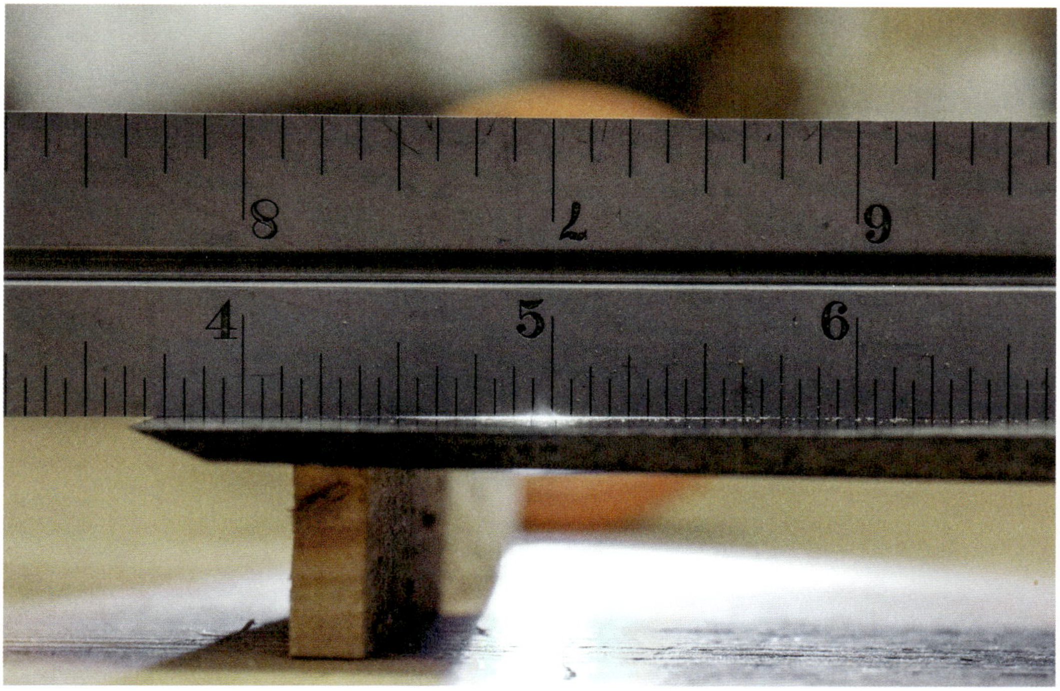
4
5
6

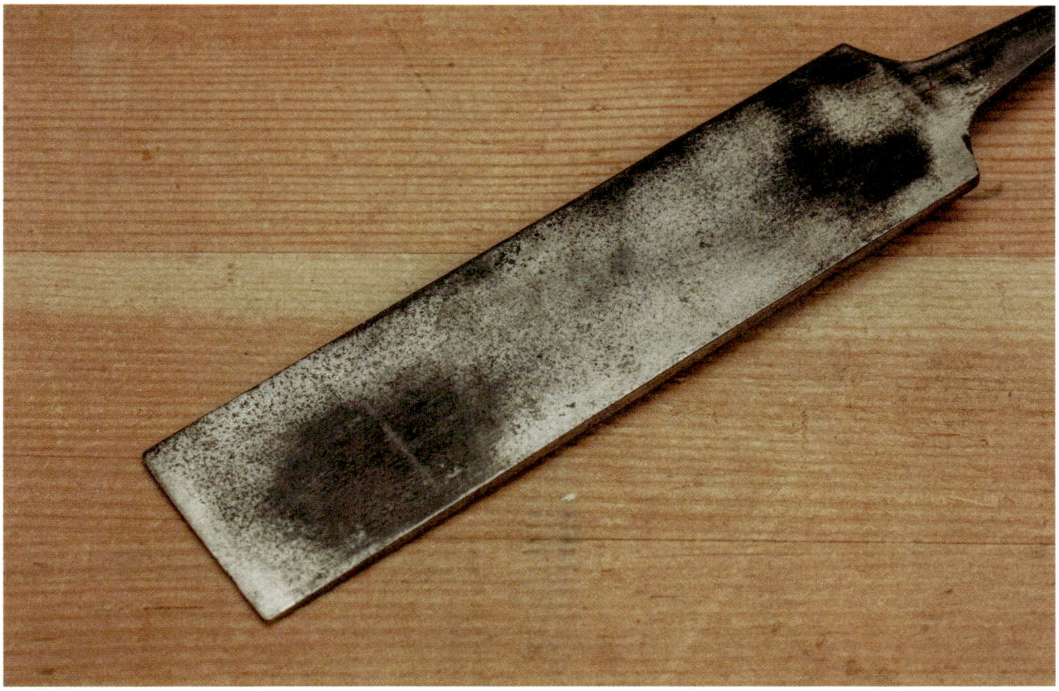

steel, to hit the temperatures needed to optimize the qualities of the steel, and to do all of this without the weld failing, is a matter of highly skilled labor. Given these barriers to automation, it's far easier to make the tool with a single piece of tool steel. And that seems to be the choice Western toolmakers made.

Japanese toolmakers, on the other hand, make laminated tools today by a variety of methods. They have found ways to automate parts of this method, such as using trip hammers instead of hammering by hand. Prices can be kept down by paying less attention to details, such as not grinding the shoulders of a chisel to a high degree of refinement. Higher-quality Japanese tools are priced to reflect the skilled craftsmanship that goes into the making of a tool, like how a custom piece of fine furniture should be priced accordingly. Finally, the Japanese government has seen fit to support traditional methods and crafts, including Japanese tool making, to a degree that is not seen in the Western world.

It is arguable, then, that the difference between Japanese and Western tools isn't a difference of East vs. West. It's a matter of traditional tool-making methods vs. compromises in the service of modernization. Experience shows that edge tools made with a lamination of harder steel to a softer steel backing perform better in terms of edge retention and ease of sharpening than edge tools made with a single piece of steel, where compromises need to be made in terms of best performance. It's easy to see why these compromises were made, however, in that it resulted in the ability to make cheaper tools, even if they weren't better.

For me, the most fascinating aspect about the story of forge-welded laminated tools is that both Japanese and Western blacksmiths seemed to develop this process in parallel and come to the same conclusions as to the best method of making tools. The implication is that these two woodworking traditions have more in common than it may seem, which supports my original assumption that Japanese and Western woodworkers have always had the same goals – to use sharpened metal to shape wood as efficiently as possible. And in today's world, that's a lesson worth keeping in mind. ◆

ENDNOTES

1. I wrote more about this in "It Comes Down to the Cut," *Popular Woodworking Magazine* Issue 199, October 2012, 68.
2. I should note that there is an alternative method of making chisels and plane blades that incorporates crucible powdered metal (CPM) technology. In this method, the various components of steel are turned into fine powder, mixed, injection-molded, and sintered to make the final project. As it turns out, this method also can create very fine carbides that are nearly as small as the ones in forge-welded laminated tools. Woodworkers who have compared CPM steel tools to Japanese tools feel that these two types of tools have similar edge-holding and sharpening characteristics, although the advantage still seems to be with Japanese tools.

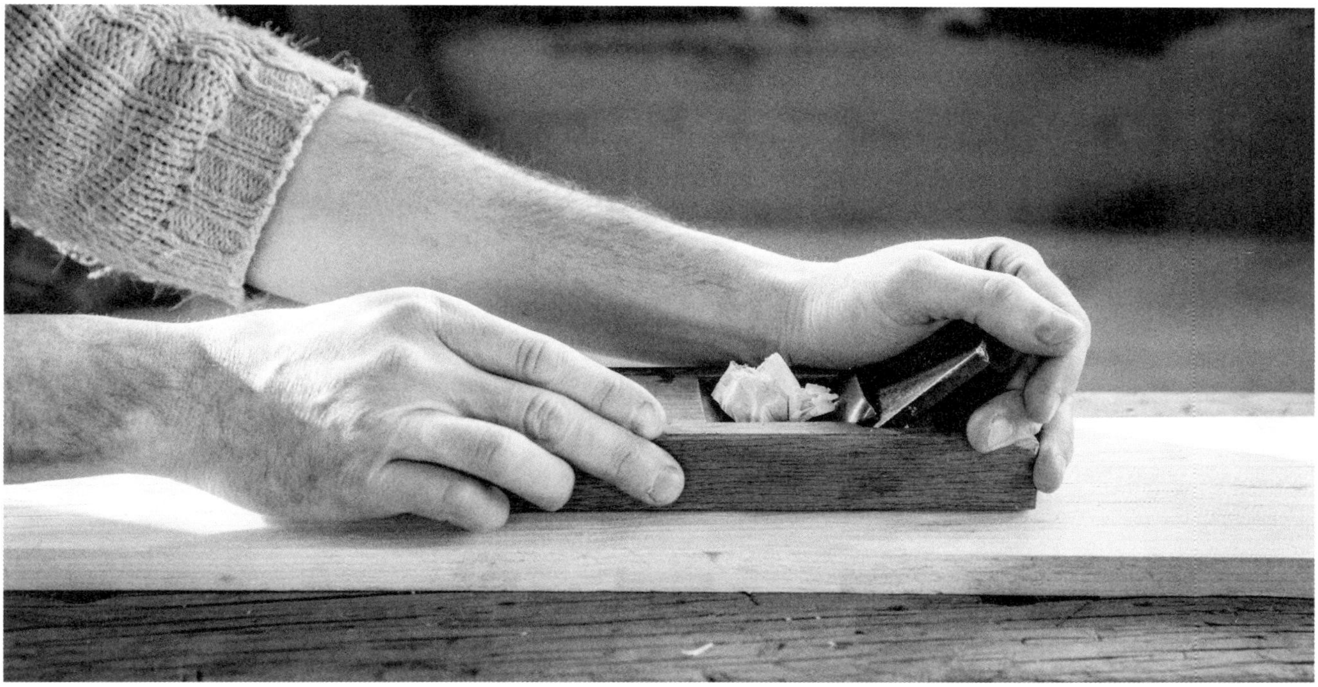

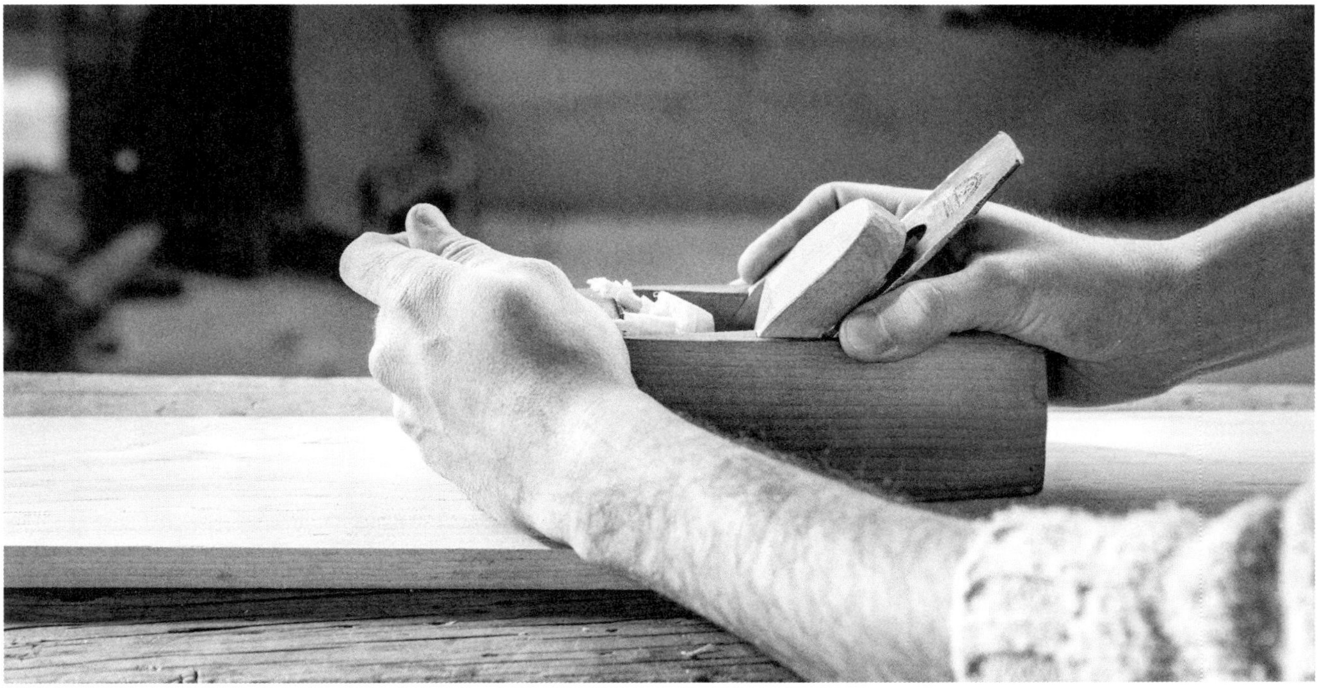

"Man is most free when his tools are proportionate to his needs."

— Sōetsu Yanagi, *The Unknown Craftsman*

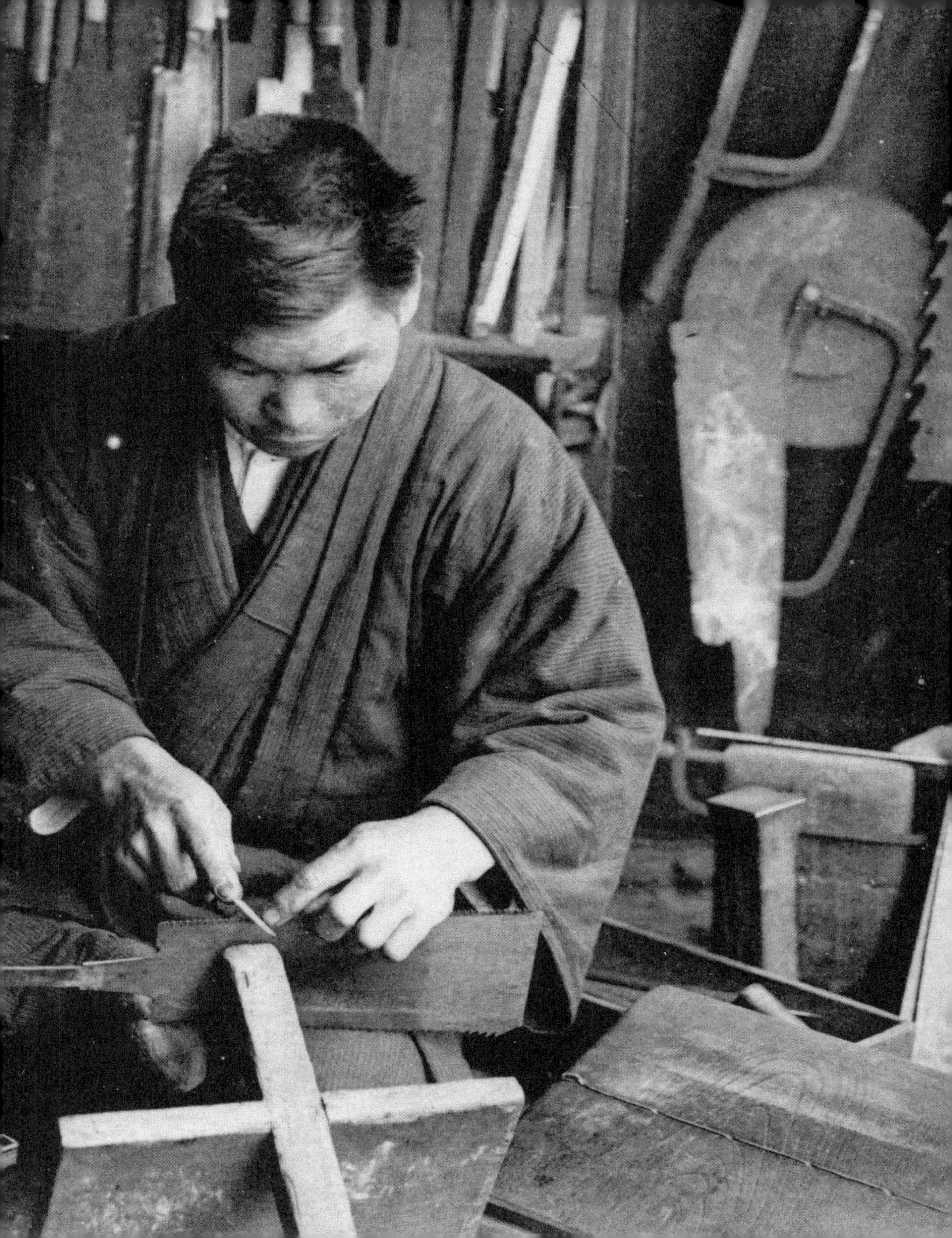

Desk with drawers and tiger-paw shaped legs. Joseon Dynasty, 19th century. Joseon. 31.0 × 73.0 cm. Courtesy of Japan Folk Crafts Museum.

The Unknown Craftsman. By Sōetsu Yanagi. Kodansha USA. 2013. 230 pages.

Reviewed by Arsenios Hill

Of the many books I've read on craft, none are like Sōetsu Yanagi's *The Unknown Craftsman*. It reads like a sacred text, and my copy has been highlighted and annotated more than any other of my craft books. The subtitle, "A Japanese Insight into Beauty," hints at his focus. Throughout the book, Yanagi articulates his unique philosophy of craft by interweaving ideas about beauty and craft inspired by his own culture with his earlier study of Western thinkers such as John Ruskin and William Morris, as well as the craft culture he encountered among the Koreans. This is not a how-to book. This is a book about ideas – a book for the contemplative craftsman. It is an exploration of the cultural and spiritual context in which beautiful and useful crafts are created.

Although the book has a strong spiritual element, for Yanagi the physical and spiritual work together, in tandem, to foster beauty. The beginning of *The Unknown Craftsman* contains 76 pages of photographs of various craft items to illustrate Yanagi's ideas, and he refers to them throughout the book. In a lengthy and interesting introduction, renowned potter Bernard Leach, also the translator, describes his friendship with Yanagi and explains key points of his philosophy. The rest of the book is an elaboration of Yanagi's ideas, experiences, and philosophies. Though he writes from a Japanese Buddhist perspective, the author draws from other traditions, including Christianity, and the reader will quickly recognize the universality of the principles he writes about.

I first encountered *The Unknown Craftsman* through Instagram when a fellow craftsman shared a story from the book about Yanagi's visit to a Korean village of woodturners. Yanagi was surprised to find them turning dripping-wet green wood. Confused, Yanagi asked one of them, "'Why do you use such green material? Cracks will come out pretty soon!' 'What does it matter?' was the calm answer. I was amazed by this Zen monk-like response. I felt sweat on my forehead. Yet I dared to ask him, 'How can you use something that leaks?' 'Just mend it,' was his simple answer. With amazement I discovered that they mend them so artistically and beautifully that the cracked piece seems better than the perfect one....What is human perfection after all? Why should one reject the perfect in favor of the imperfect?...The perfect is static and regulated, cold and hard....Beauty must have some room, must be associated with freedom....Love of the irregular is a sign of the basic quest for freedom."

This story captures much of the spirit and essence of Yanagi's book, his passion for the process of creating beautiful handmade crafts, and his conviction that the heart must guide the head and the hand.

Though Yanagi has a particular love for ceramics, he includes many other crafts in his writing. According to him, handmade crafts should be inexpensive and made to be used by everyday people. They should also be representative of the particular culture from which they were produced. He strongly criticizes the sterile uniformity and perfection of machine-made items in favor of the subtle imperfections of hand work. Community involvement is also important to Yanagi, and he harkens back to the craft guilds of the Middle Ages as an example of the ideal communal nature of craft culture.

I grew up among the indigenous peoples in the Amazon rainforest, in the very type of craft community Yanagi describes. Though this community lacked many of the tools modern craftsmen consider essential, they made articles of stunning beauty and skill. Because of that experience, each page of this book deeply resonated with me as Yanagi insightfully put into words the beauty, meaning, and significance of traditional folk crafts. Yanagi contends that these handmade crafts are a product of the authentic human hand and spirit, and it is this quality that can help to enrich our own lives and culture today. His work is deeply philosophical, but it also elevates traditional crafts to a place of respect and dignity, giving them worth in our modern Western context. It is this particular genius that gives *The Unknown Craftsman* the power to inspire and guide each of us along the path of creating functional beauty in the true spirit of traditional craft. ◆

SPONSOR DIRECTORY

The following are the businesses and individuals that sponsor this edition of *Mortise & Tenon Magazine*. This Directory is a way to highlight the mutual endorsement we share with our sponsors. The bottom line: If someone is listed here it's because we support what they're doing and they support what we're doing. Everyone in this Directory has been hand-selected for high-quality and high-integrity business practice. These folks share our vision to celebrate historic furniture making and offer tools, training, and inspiration to aid your creative life.

If you are looking for recommendations of suppliers or makers, we recommend you look here first. We happily endorse and support these companies and hope you will, too.

Auriou

Forge de Saint Juery is the home of Auriou Toolworks in south-west France where they free forge tools for artists for the precision shaping of wood, stone & plaster. Auriou are world famous for the quality and performance of their hand stitched rasps & rifflers in particular but also make a fine range of carving and guilding tools.

www.auriou.fr

Benchcrafted
Fine Vises & Tools

Fine vises for traditional workbenches, bench appliances from the golden age of woodworking, and unique tools for the modern hand tool enthusiast. Entirely made in the US of A.

www.benchcrafted.com
info@benchcrafted.com

Blackburn Tools

Blackburn Tools is dedicated to the craft and art of saws and other handtools, and furnishes tools and support to woodworkers interested in the same. Focused on saw parts and kits, with comprehensive saw building instructions and resources freely available on our website.

blackburntools.com
isaac@blackburntools.com

Blue Spruce Toolworks
Hand tools for your finest work

We started Blue Spruce Toolworks with a singular vision: Hand crafted tools that are not only aesthetically beautiful, but are also a joy to use in the creative process. It is our hope that our tools - like the pieces you create with them - will be passed down and enjoyed for generations to come.

www.bluesprucetoolworks.com

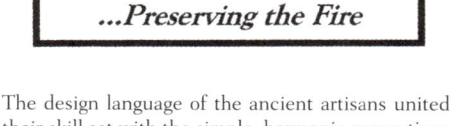

By Hand & Eye
...Preserving the Fire

The design language of the ancient artisans united their skill set with the simple, harmonic proportions they observed in nature. Join Jim Tolpin & George Walker in their on-line "Designer's Atelier" to learn this timeless language of the artisans.

www.byhandandeye.com

Charleston Woodworking School

The Charleston Woodworking School offers a blend of traditional skills & contemporary techniques producing quality furniture. Marquetry, gilding, joinery, design, restoration and more are faculty taught with the Professional Course, Continuing Education and Short Courses. VA benefits approved.

www.charlestonwoodworkingschool.com

The Colonial Homestead

The Colonial Homestead offers one of the nation's finest selections of handtools, period furniture, and artisan work. In 2017, we are adding a trade school (Colonial Homestead Artisans Guild). With over 11,000 square feet of handtools, workshop, antiques, artisanwork, fine art, and handtool classes, Colonial Homestead is a one-stop destination.

www.cohoartguild.com
330-600-9445

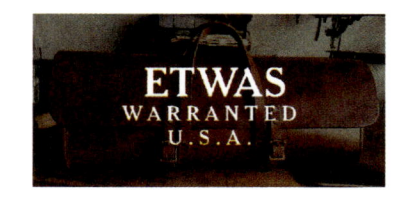

ETWAS Warranted U.S.A.

Makers of fine tool bags and custom leather cases. Proud to use the best US made and naturally vegetable tanned leather and solid metal fittings. Individually hand sewn in Vermont, USA.

www.etwasbags.com

Fine Tool Journal

The *Fine Tool Journal* is a quarterly magazine for the user and avid collector of fine hand tools, including articles on tool history, use, and preservation. Each issue also features an absentee auction with choice selections of user and collectible hand tools.

www.finetooljournal.net
finetoolj@gmail.com

Fine WoodWorking

For over 40 years, *Fine Woodworking* has been providing the most trusted and highest quality information on every aspect of the woodworking craft. Experienced and respected woodworkers share their extensive knowledge with an audience of all skill levels, whether they are novices or advanced woodworkers building the most challenging projects.

www.finewoodworking.com

Furniture Institute of Massachusetts

The Furniture Institute of Massachusetts is dedicated to excellence in the art of classical woodworking techniques and functional contemporary furniture design and construction. We have a program designed to teach the traditional woodworking techniques that have for centuries proven successful in building the world's masterpieces. Full-time, nights, weekends & summer programs available.

http://www.furnituremakingclasses.com

Grandpa's Little Farm
~Reconditioned Vintage Handtools~

Tool restoration was just part of a small hobby farm that we started in 2009. We specialize in user woodworking tools, specializing in braces, bits, and metal bodied planes, but will try to track down special items on request. We take pride in spending time with each client and completely warranty each item we ship. And coming soon will be our own product line of apparel and tool care items!

www.grandpaslittlefarm.com   253-536-0197

Highland Woodworking

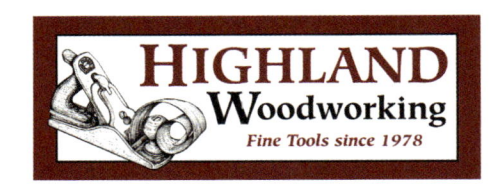

A family-owned business, Highland Woodworking has served woodworkers with fine tools and education since 1978. Always committed to quality and value, Highland is well known for providing reliable advice on the purchase and use of woodworking tools.

http://www.highlandwoodworking.com
(800) 241-6748

Horton Brasses, Inc.

Since 1936, Horton Brasses has been making period correct reproduction hardware. Our patterns are exact copies of antique originals and we employ traditional production methods wherever possible. The addition of the Londonderry Brasses collection means we have more selection and capability than ever before.

www.horton-brasses.com

Inside Passage

Our small school provides craft education for the aspiring amateur. We offers not a way to make a living, but a way of life. "If I were starting my life today as a craftsman, and needed to learn what matters the most; my choice would be Inside Passage school."
- James Krenov

insidepassage.ca
1.877.943.9663
robert@insidepassage.ca

Lee Valley & Veritas

Lee Valley and Veritas® are Canadian family-owned businesses that have been supplying high quality woodworking, gardening, and home products since 1978.

http://leevalley.com
1- 800-267-8735

Liberty Tool Company / Davistown Museum

The Liberty Tool Co. is the largest branch of the Jonesport Wood Company, which also has locations in Hulls Cove (The Tool Barn) and Searsport (Captain Tinkham's Emporium). The Davistown Museum is a regional tool, art, and history museum that chronicles tools and the impact they have on the individuals and societies using them.

http://www.libertytoolco.com
http://davistownmuseum.org   (207) 589-4771

Lie-Nielsen Toolworks, Inc.

Our Mission is to design and create beautiful heirloom-quality hand tools that inspire woodworkers and other artisans. Through exceptional support and education, our customers receive the same personal attention we put into our tools.

http://lie-nielsen.com
(800) 327-2520

The Maine Coast Craft School

Offering classes in traditional green wood working at our off-grid, hand-built school in Bristol, Maine. Distributors of Hans Karlsson, Svante Djärv & US made, hand-forged tools for working green wood.

www.mainecoastcraft.com

Mary May's School of Traditional Woodcarving

My online video school teaches a variety of traditional woodcarving techniques, focusing on period furniture details and classical ornamentation. To keep the instruction fresh and unique, a new HD video is added every week.

http://www.marymaycarving.com/carvingschool
(843) 200-9469

M-WTCA

Studying, Preserving, and Sharing Knowledge of Tools

Please check out our website for information and to join. Our meetings are one of the best places to find the hand tools you are looking for, as well as folks who know the history behind them.

www.MWTCA.org

North Bennet St. School

AN EDUCATION IN CRAFTSMANSHIP

A life of proven skills, artful solutions, and superior craftsmanship – built by hand. Full-Time programs and Continuing Education classes in furniture making and fine woodworking. Master faculty and an inspiring community located in Boston's historic North End. Financial aid and veterans' benefits available.

http://nbss.edu/furniture
617.227.0155

North House Folk School

ENRICHING LIVES & BUILDING COMMUNITY THROUGH TRADITIONAL NORTHERN CRAFT

North House is an educational non-profit located on the shore of Lake Superior in Minnesota. Our mission is to enrich lives and build community by teaching traditional northern crafts in a student-centered learning environment that inspires the hands, the heart and the mind. Furniture building, woodturning and beyond.
www.northhouse.org
218-387-9762

Plate 11 Workbench Co.

Plate 11 Woodworking makes and teaches classes on making Roubo workbenches, tool chests, shave horses and any other piece of woodwork you see on their Instagram feed (@markbuildsit).

http://www.plate11.com

Port Townsend School of Woodworking

Our mission is to inspire a lifelong passion for craftsmanship through education in woodworking and traditional building trades. Located in the beautiful Pacific Northwest, we offer weekend, week-long, and intensive classes taught by expert woodworkers and educators. As one alum put it: "Skilled instructors, sharp tools and a to-die-for location."

www.ptwoodschool.org
360.344.4455

RareWoods.US

RareWoods.US offers over 165 different types of exotic woods through its eBay store. Specializing in African Blackwood, Pink Ivory-wood to the rarest Rosewoods from every corner of the globe. Below market prices with deep shipping discounts to better serve the customer. Travis is an experienced woodworker with knowledge of craft and wood expertise, helping his customers to choose the best products.

http://stores.shop.ebay.covm/rarewoodsus
@rarewoods.us

Red Rose Reproductions

Red Rose Reproductions primary focus is reproducing 18th century tools including various side escapement planes, spill planes, and panel raising planes, along with other hand tools. We offer beech billets and tapered irons for those wishing to build their own planes. We also offer wood vice screws of various sizes from Acer-Ferrous Toolworks.

http://redrosereproductions.com
dan@redrosereproductions.com

Sawyer Made

At Sawyer Made, George carries on the legacy of his father, David Sawyer. Small classes are held at the family homestead in rural Vermont with a focus on skill building and taking the time to get it right. Students use traditional hand tools to rive, carve and turn every element of a chair that will last for generations.

www.sawyermade.com
802.249.6300

Society of American Period Furniture Makers

Society of American Period Furniture Makers: dedicated to the understanding, education, and appreciation of American period furniture.

www.sapfm.org
membership@sapfm.org

Southwest School of Woodworking

The Southwest School of Woodworking is the only comprehensive woodworking school in Arizona. We are dedicated to the preservation of our craft. We stress traditional hand tool techniques, machine tools are also introduced to round out the experience. Classes run from the beginner to advanced.

http://www.sw-sw.org
480-734-0274

Sterling Tool Works

Sterling Tool Works is inspired by artisans that create fine work. Our vision is to bring highly refined tools to market that are both beautiful, functional, and therefore, inspire and enable artisans to produce their very best work.

http://sterlingtoolworks.com
chris@sterlingtoolworks.com

The Unplugged Woodshop

The Unplugged Woodshop is hand tools and inspiration, education and design. Inspiring you to slow down and work smarter with your hands and heart.

http://theunpluggedwoodshop.com
tomfidgen@yahoo.ca

Vesper Tools

Finest Hand Tools for all Woodworkers. Made by hand in Australia since 1998 with unerring quality, Vesper Tools specializes in the foundation tools of precision measuring and marking for your woodworking pleasure.

http://vespertools.com.au
Shipped all over the world.

Walke Moore Tools

With a focus on producing tools that are not readily available today, Walke Moore Tools is committed to designing and manufacturing the highest quality hand tools available using only the finest materials.

http://walkemooretools.com
info@walkemoortools.com

The Woodwright's School

The Woodwright's School is a place devoted to the powerful pleasures of hand tool woodworking! Learn from instructors Roy Underhill, Bill Anderson, Elia Bizzarri, and more.

http://woodwrightschool.com
89 A. Hillsboro St. Pittsboro, NC

COLOPHON

Mortise & Tenon Magazine is set in Fairfield, a contemporary typeface consciously tethered to the Venetian Old Face tradition. Fairfield was designed in 1940 by Rudolph Ruzicka, whose philosophy of tasteful design was grounded in the truth that "type is made to be read" and that the reader "expects nothing but to be left in optical ease while he pursues his reading."

This publication was printed and perfect bound at Royle Printing in Sun Prairie, Wisconsin, using 70# Finch Opaque uncoated paper.